iPhone 12

User Manual

A Comprehensive Step By Step Guide With Ultimate Pictorial Illustrations To Navigate Your New Device And Actual Slo-Mo To Master Your New IOS 14

BY

West Liberty

Table of Contents

CHAPTER ONE

KNOW YOUR NEW IPHONE(WELCOME)

Take Your Best Shot

Take great shots with your iPhone in any situation. From candid photos to studio-quality portraits - you can take them all with an iPhone camera.

Let It Be Yours

Customize your home screen background, add gadgets to quickly view important information, organize apps, and more.

Stay In Touch

Use your iPhone to connect with friends and family in new ways.

Be Good

iPhone can help you keep track of health and activity patterns, introduce a bedtime routine, and more.

Supported iPhone Models

This manual will help you get started with the iPhone and discover all the surprising things it can do in iOS 14.4 that is compatible with the following models:

iPhone 12 mini, iPhone 12 Pro iPhone X, iPhone SE (2nd generation)-iPhone 8, iPhone 8 Plus, iPhone 7, iPhone 7 Plus, iPhone 6s, iPhone 6s Plus, iPhone SE (1st generation) If your model supports it, you can update it to the latest iOS software.

To view the model and software version of your iPhone, go to Settings> General> Business Card.

iPhone NUTS AND BOLTS

Set up mobile service on iPhone

For a mobile connection on the iPhone, you need a SIM from the operator; contact your network operator to set up the mobile package.

5G networks are available in iPhone 12 models.

Your iPhone can connect to your mobile carrier's network with a physical nano-SIM. iPhone XS, iPhone XR, and later support dual SIM cards using one physical nano-SIM and one eSIM (not available in all countries or regions).

See ways to use dual sim:

- ✓ Use one sim number for business and another sim number for personal calls.
- ✓ Add a local data package when traveling to another country or region.
- ✓ You have separate voice and data plans.

Note: Your iPhone must be unlocked to use two different parentheses.

Install A Physical Nano-Sim

1.Insert a paper clip or SIM card remover into a small hole in the SIM tray and then slide it toward iPhone to eject the tray.

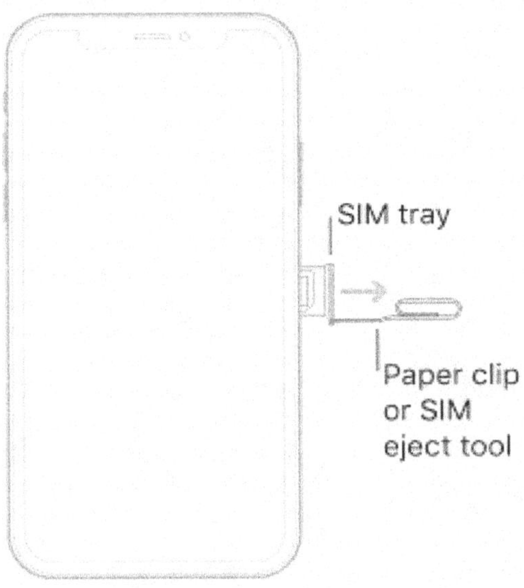

A tool for removing the clip or SIM card is inserted into the small hole on the right side of the iPhone to remove and remove the tray.

2.Remove the tray from the iPhone.

3.Insert the nano-SIM into the tray. The angular angle determines the correct orientation.

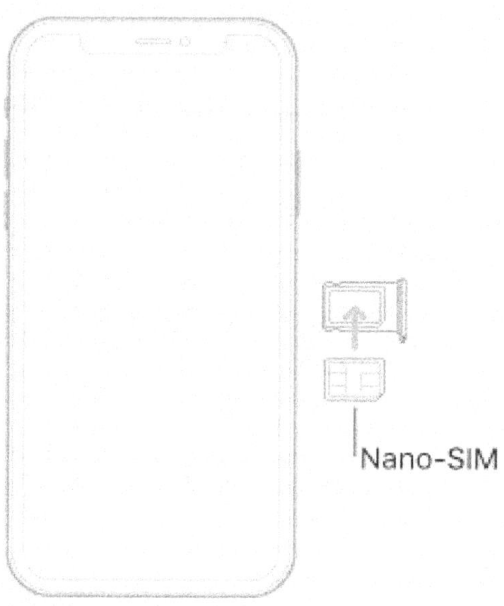

4.Insert the tray back into the iPhone.

5.If you have already set a PIN on the nano-SIM, enter it carefully if necessary.

WARNING: Never attempt to guess the SIM code. Wrong guessing can permanently lock the SIM card and you will not be able to make calls or use mobile data through your network operator until you get a new SIM card.

Manage Your Mobile Packages For Dual Sim

During setup on dual SIM models, you can choose how iPhone uses each line. To change or adjust the settings do this:

1.Go to Settings> Mobile Network.

2.Do the following:

-Touch Cellular Data and select the default row. To allow iPhone to use any line, depending on network covered and accessibility

Switch on allow Cellular Data.

If data roaming is turned on and you are outside the country or region covered by the network, you may have to pay for roaming.

- Tap Default voice line, and then select a line.

-Tap the line below the cellular packets, then change settings such as the cellular packet label, Wi-Fi dialing (if available from your network operator), calls to other devices, or the SIM code. The bookmark is displayed on the phone, messages, and contacts.

When using a dual SIM card, note the following:

✓ Wi-Fi dialing must be turned on for the line to receive calls while the other line is used for the call.

If you receive a call on one line while the other is used for the call and a Wi-Fi connection is not available, iPhone uses the mobile data of the line that was used for the call to answer the call on the other line. Fees may be charged.

The line used for the call must be able to use the data in the cell data settings (either as a default or as a non-default line with cell data switching enabled) to receive the second call.

> ➤ If you do not turn on Wi-Fi calls for a line, all incoming phone calls on that line (including emergency calls) are routed directly to voicemail (if available from your network operator) when the other line is in use; you will not receive notifications of missed calls.

If you set a conditional call to divert (if available from your network operator) from one line to another when the line is busy or not working,

calls will not be diverted to voicemail; contact your network operator for settings information.

> ➤ If you are calling from another device, such as a Mac, and transferring it via the iPhone with a dual SIM card, the call is made using the default voice line.

- If you start an SMS / MMS conversation with one line, you cannot switch the conversation to another line;

you need to delete the conversation and start a new conversation with another line. You can also charge extra if you send SMS / MMS attachments on a line that is not selected for mobile data.

- Instant Hotspot and Personal Hotspot use the line selected for mobile data.

GETTING SET UP

Turn on and set up iPhone

Switch on and set your latest iPhone over an Internet connection. You can also set up the iPhone by connecting it to a computer.

Data can be transfer to the new iPhone through another iPad, iPod touch, or android device.

Get Ready To Set Up

To make the installation as smooth as possible, enable the following elements:

1. . Internet connection via Wi-Fi (you may need a network name and password) or a mobile data service via a mobile operator

2. . Your Apple ID and password; if you don't have an Apple ID, you can create one during installation

3. . Your credit or debit card account information to add to Apple Pay during installation

4. . Previous backup of iPhone or device if you are transferring data to a new device

5. . Your Android device if you are downloading Android content

Turn On And Set Up iPhone

1.Press and hold the side key either to sleep or wake and wait until the Apple logo appears.

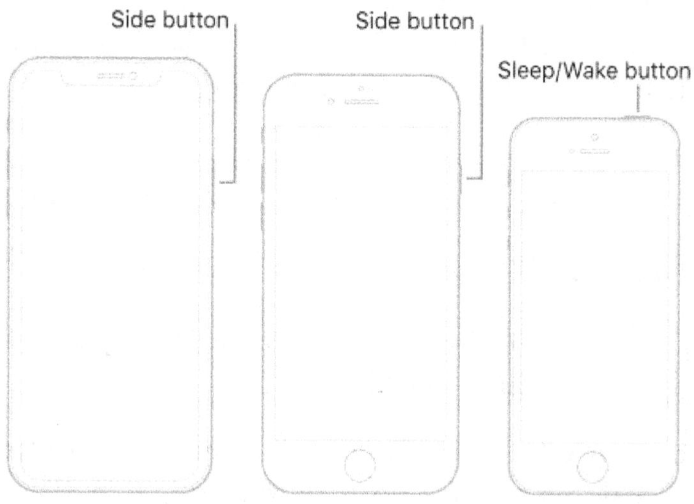

If iPhone doesn't turn on, you may need to charge the battery.

2.Do one of the following:

- Touch Setup manually and follow the on-screen setup instructions.
- If you have another iPhone, iPad, or iPod touch with iOS 11, iPad 13, or later, you can set up a new device automatically with a quick start.

Zoom in on two devices and follow the onscreen instructions to securely copy many of the iCloud key settings, settings, and berths.

You can then restore other data and content from your iCloud backup to your new device.

=If the two devices have iOS 12.4, iPad 13, or later, you can move all data wirelessly from the former device to the new one. Keep the devices near to each other and connect them until the migration process is complete.

You can also transfer data over a wired connection between devices.

If you are blind or partially sighted, press the side button three times (on the iPhone with Face ID) or click the Home button three times to switch on Voiceover.

You can also click twice on the screen with three fingers to turn on zoom.

Move from Android Device to iPhone

When you set up your new iPhone for the first time, you can automatically and securely move data from your Android device.

Note: You can only use the Move to iOS app when you first set up iPhone.

When you are done setting up and want to Move to iOS, you have to delete iPhone and start all over or move the data manually.

1.On your Android 4.0 or later device, see the Apple Support Article Move from Android to iPhone, iPad, or iPod touch and download the Move to iOS app.

2.Do the following on your iPhone:

. Follow the setup assistant.

. On the Apps & Data field, click transfer data from Android.

3.Do the following on your Android device:

. Turn on Wi-Fi.

. Open the Move to iOS app.

. Follow the on-screen instructions.

Connect Your iPhone To The Internet

Connect your iPhone to the Internet through an available Wi-Fi or mobile network.

Connect your iPhone to a Wi-Fi network

1.Go to Settings> Wi-Fi and then turn on Wi-Fi.

2.Touch one of the following:

. Network: Enter a password, if required.

. Other: Join a hidden network. Enter the hidden network name, security type, and password.

When you see Wi-Fi at the top of the screen, the Wi-Fi network is connected. The iPhone reconnects when you return to the same location.

Join A Personal Contact Point

. If your iPad (Wi-Fi + mobile phone) or other iPhone has a personal access point, you can use its mobile Internet connection.

. Go to Settings> Wi-Fi, and then select the name of the device that shares the personal access point. If iPhone asks for a password, enter the password.

Connect IPhone to Your Mobile Network

Your iPhone automatically connects to your carrier's mobile data network if Wi-Fi isn't available. If iPhone fails to connect, check this:

1.Make sure the SIM card is activated and unlocked. See Set up a mobile service on iPhone.

2.Go to Settings> Mobile Network.

3.Make sure your mobile data is turned on. For dual SIM models, tap Cellular Data, and then confirm the selected row. (You can only select one row for mobile data.)

When you need an Internet connection, iPhone does all of the following until it connects:

. Attempt to connect to the latest available Wi-Fi network

. Displays a list of Wi-Fi networks within range and connects to the selected one

. It connects to your mobile operator's mobile data network

Sign in with Your Apple Id

If you did not log in during the installation, do the following:

1.Go to Settings.

2.Touch iPhone Login.

3.Enter your Apple ID and password.

But if you don't have the ID, then make one.

4.If you are protecting your account with two-factor authentication, enter a six-digit verification code.

If you have forgotten your Apple ID or password, visit the Apple ID Recovery website.

Change Apple ID settings

1.Go to Settings> [your name].

2.Do one of the following:

- Update your contact information
- change the password
- Manage family sharing

Change Your iCloud Settings

1.Go to Settings> [your name]> iCloud.

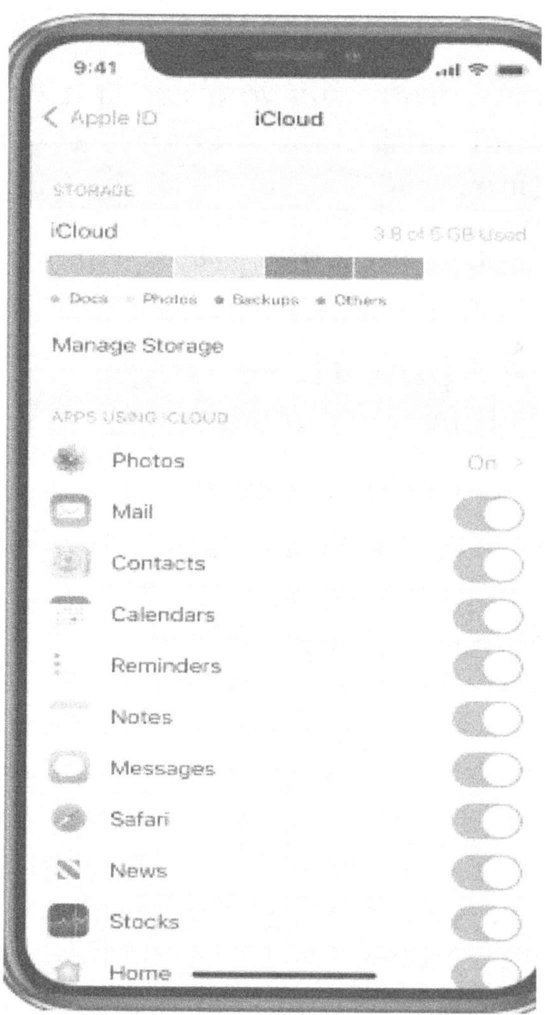

2.Do one of the following:

＋ . See the storage status in iCloud.

✦ . Upgrade your iCloud memory - tap Memory management> Change storage plan.

✦ . Switch on the features you want to use, such as photos, mail, contacts, and messages.

Download The User Guide from Apple Books

1.Open the Books app.

2.Touch Search, and then enter the "iPhone User Guide."

3.Press get, and then wait for it to download

iPhone SETTING

Change These Settings

1. Don't want or want 5G coverage? Turn it off

Apple's four iPhone 12 models are the first from the company to offer support for 5G, mostly a faster and more reliable cellular connection.

As operators continue to deploy their 5G networks, some iPhone 12 owners (myself included) will have to wait for 5G access.

Apple announces the Smart 12 feature of the iPhone 12, which will automatically switch between 4G LTE and 5G networks without you having to know or do so depending on how you use the iPhone 12.

Automatic switching is part of the effort to extend battery life. However, you may find that your iPhone 12's battery drains faster than before. Then switch off faster 5G speeds.

You can turn on 5G again and again whenever you want or when the service in your area improves.

To turn off 5G on iPhone 12 and force it to always use 4G LTE, even if you have 5G coverage, open the Settings app, then open Cellular> Cellular Data Options> Voice & Data, and tap LTE.

If you want your iPhone 12 to only use a 5G connection when available, you can select 5G On.

2. Set exactly how much data is used for the 5G connection

If you are satisfied with the 5G performance, you need to check the network setting. Go to Settings to Mobile Data Options to Data Mode, where you'll find three different options: Enable data in 5G mode, Standard and Low.

Although there are short descriptions under three different settings, they do not give a complete picture for the first option.

Apple's support document says, allowing more data on 5G, you get high-quality video and FaceTime calls.

This also means your phone can download software updates, stream Apple TV and Apple Music, and allow third-party developers to improve their apps as well.

3. iOS 14 has changed the incoming call alert revert it

Before iOS 14, whenever your iPhone is unlocked and used - for example, to check email - and when someone calls, the incoming call screen takes over the entire screen.

Sure, it bothers you, but you were also well aware that the phone was ringing.

Starting with iOS 14, however, Apple changed the incoming call query to be more like a regular alert.

This is a small notification that appears at the top of the screen when you use your phone.

Several times, I almost missed a call because I turned off the alert as another annoying notification that didn't immediately need my attention.

To return an incoming call alert in full-screen mode, go to Settings> Phone> Incoming calls and tap Fullscreen mode

4. Display the complete notifications on the lock screen

If this device is your foremost experience with Apple's Face ID technology, you'll notice that you don't see the contents of new alerts and notifications on the lock screen.

For example, instead of seeing who sent you a text message and what it says, you'll only see a general warning about the message.

By default, Apple's Face ID technology will hide the alert until you unlock it.

It's a privacy feature that I enjoy the most, but at the same time, I understand how boring it can be (and we've also heard some complaints from readers and family members).

To change how the notifications are shown on the lock screen, go to Settings> Notifications> Show preview and select Always. Conversely, you can select Never it will not show again on the lock screen.

5. You may want to turn off this camera feature for now for now

Each iPhone 12 model has received modest camera updates, including the ability to record HDR or high dynamic range videos with Dolby Vision. Yes. I shot a video with the iPhone 12 Pro a few nights ago and I said wow. But the problem is not every app or service will work with HDR videos.

At the moment, this means that when you upload a video to Facebook or Instagram, the colorful video you see on the iPhone 12 will look too bright and will lose some of its magic. Developers will need to update their programs to accept HDR video, but even then, the person watching the video will need a capable device to see the difference in HDR. For Apple devices that include the iPhone 8 or later, the iPad Air 2020, the second-generation iPad Pro, and some Macs.

So what can you do? Well, you have several options:

a) You can turn off HDR video by going to Settings> Camera> Movie Recording and setting the switch next to HDR Video to Off. In the future, all videos will be recorded at the usual dynamic range, and you won't have any problems sharing or editing.

b) Let HDR Video switch on, but if you want to share the video like Facebook, use the Picture or photo app instead of using the Facebook app and then uploading it there. Using photos, your iPhone will automatically convert the video to SDR and transfer it. When you send a video to another iPhone user, Apple will determine if their iPhone, iPad, or Mac is HDR-compatible with Dolby Vision. Otherwise, Apple will automatically convert the video.

c) If you leave HDR Video on and need to edit it, you can use Apple's iMovie app or the Photos app built into your iPhone. If necessary, you can even use iMovie to export videos as SDRs.

6. Avoid crowds on the home screen

With the release of iOS 14, iPhone users have more options and control over the look of the home screen than ever before.

For example, the new application library acts as a program tray and allows you to remove programs from the Home screen without deleting them.

Hell, you can even customize the look of your phone with a variety of app icons and accessories. It's very similar to Android, and there's nothing wrong with that.

However, if you don't want new apps to go directly to the app library, where you'll forget to visit them after a day or two,

Go to Settings> Home screen and select Add to home screen only on the screen or in the app library.

7. Use a luxurious wallpaper

Another home screen setting you need to make includes wallpaper. Apple has added some of its wallpapers to the latest updates with a pretty cool move.

Open the Settings app on iPhone and select Wallpaper from the list. Make sure the "Dark Appearance Darkens Background" switch is on under two thumbnail previews of your background.

Now tap Select new wallpaper and select Stills or Live

8. Turn on dark mode. You won't be sorry

Speaking of dark mode, if you don't want to adjust the screen brightness multiple times, you can use the phone's dedicated dark mode, which has been proven to save battery life.

Dark mode changes the white background in applications more often than a black background. In return, your phone may save battery power due to darker colors.

To switch it on, go to Settings> Display and brightness and select Dark at the top of the screen.

9. Turn on Do Not Disturb mode

I often wonder how I slept through the night before. Now Do Not Disturb system was added to iOS. When the Do Not Disturb feature is turned on, it mutes all alerts on your iPhone, either by using a set schedule or on-demand.

Notifications will still be waiting for you when you wake up in the morning, but by turning on DND, your phone will not beep or beep about Facebook updates and work emails.

If you're worried that someone needs to get you in an emergency, you can tell DND to ring the phone when you receive multiple calls from the same number.

You can also choose to always allow calls from contacts you've added to your favorites.

10. Make it easier to read the text on the screen

With a few taps on the iPhone screen, you can adjust the font size for easier reading.

Launch Settings to Display & Brightness to Text Size, adjust the slider until you are ok with the font size.

For a little extra look, you can include bold text (just below the Text Size button)

11. Add an alternate face ID

Apple's Face ID feature constantly teaches and examines different aspects of your face with each scan.

If you're trying to get a Face ID to recognize you all the time, try a different look.

Go to Settings> Face ID and Password> enter your PIN> Set up an alternate look and go through the face registration process again.

12. Disable automatic lighting for longer battery life

The brightness level of your iPhone's screen can greatly affect battery life. By default, IOS will automatically adjust the brightness of the screen according to the amount of light detected by the ambient sensor. However, if you want to take full control, you can disable auto-exposure, which means that the brightness level you set will remain the moment you adjust it again.

Go to Settings> Accessibility> Screen and the text size and you'll find a switch to turn off auto-brightness at the bottom of the page.

Now, whenever you want to customize the screen, you can do so by opening the Control Center by dragging the home key up from the bottom of the screen on your device or dragging it down from the top right corner on newer iPhone devices.

13. The control center makes contact and pulls with your finger

The Control Center is a convenient place to quickly change songs, turn on airplane mode, connect to Wi-Fi, or count down, but there's much more to it. You can quickly turn on the flashlight, check the timer, or start recording the screen quickly and tap.

Customize which apps and features are available in Control Center by going to Settings> Control Center> Customize Controls.

To remove an option, tap the red minus button or add it by selecting the green add button.

WHAT IS NEW ABOUT IOS 14.3.4

Home screen widgets The widgets have been improved upon to give you much information at a glance as you add them to your home screen. Choose between different sizes and arrange them as you wish.

You can also add a Smart Stack that displays widgets based on factors such as your location, activity, or time.

Application library -The new on-screen home application library automatically organizes all your applications into one simple, easy-to-navigate view. The applications are sorted by category, and the applications you use most often are always one click away. See Application Library Research.

Compact calls- Incoming calls, FaceTime calls, and calls from third-party applications, appear in a compact and full-screen design.

App Clips -is a small app that is directed on performing a specific task like renting a bike, paying for parking, or ordering food.

You can find app clips in Safari, Maps, and Messages, or the real world using App Clip code (iOS 14.3), QR code, and NFC tags.

Translate is a new application designed for natural and simple conversations between languages.

Rotate the iPhone horizontally to enter talk mode where you can easily see both sides of the conversation.

You can also translate by voice or text, translate completely to your downloaded device, save your favorite translations, and more.

Search -Search is now one destination where you can start all searches. A new design and typing experience brings faster and more relevant results in applications, contacts, and web searches.

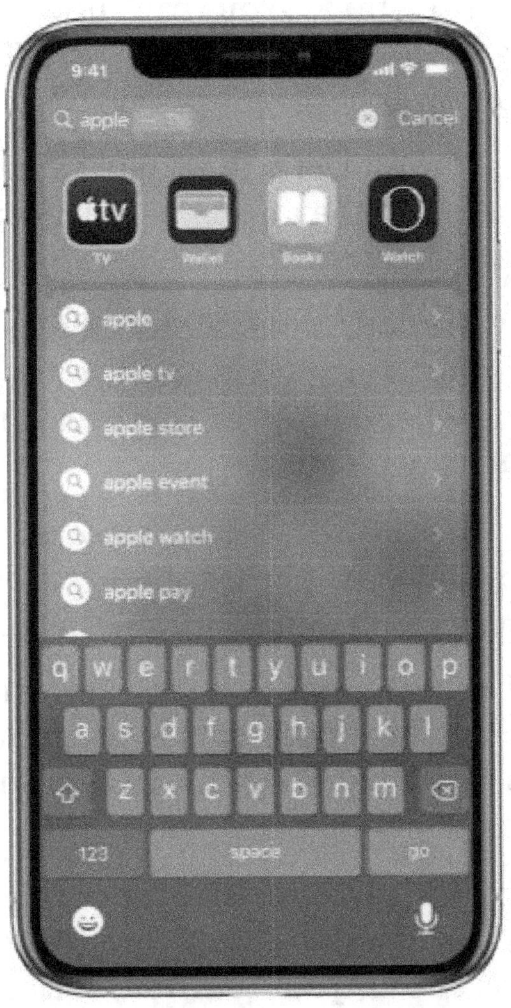

A screen showing a search query on the iPhone. At the top is the search box that contains the "apple" search text, and below it are the search results for the search text.

Picture in Picture -You can now continue watching videos or resume your FaceTime call while using another application.

Messages- Connect the most important conversations to the top of the conversation list so you can easily reach them.

In a conversation, name someone to address a message directly to them, and use the built-in replies to respond directly to a specific message in a group conversation.

Memoji- You can choose among 20 new hairstyles and headwear that reflect your hobby, your profession, and your personality.

Maps- Use the Maps to get directions for cycling using bike paths, trails, and paths. You can also see changes, busy roads, and steep hills when planning a trip.

Discover great places to eat, shop, and explore with the help of a guide. See How to Get Cycling Directions from your current location and Explore new destinations with a guide.

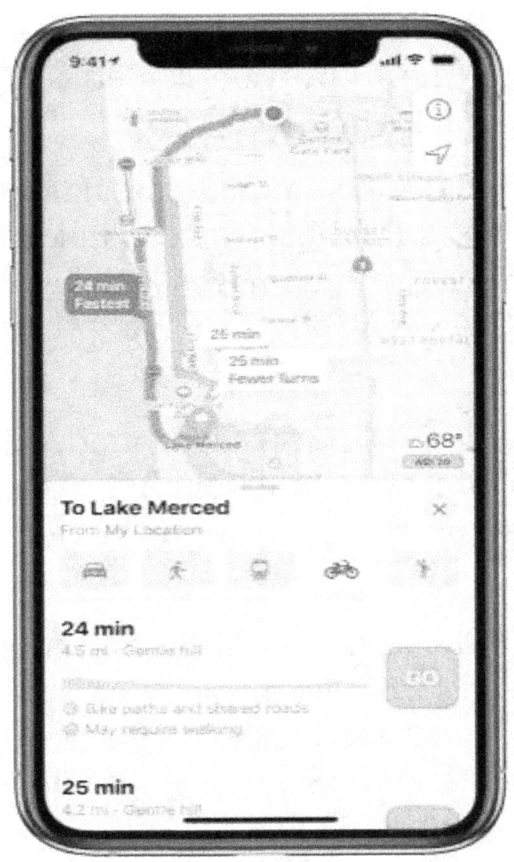

Camera-The QuickTake camcorder is now available on iPhone Xs, iPhone Xs Max, iPhone XR, and newer versions. Fast switches allow you to easily change the video resolution and frame rate in Video mode. View QuickTake Video Capture and Use Quick Switches to change video resolution and frame rate.

Night mode is available on the front selfie camera on the ultra-wide camera (0.5x) and the wide camera (1x).

Apple ProRAV (iOS 14.3) On the iPhone 12 Pro and iPhone 12 Pro Max, you can take photos in Apple ProRAV to edit images with higher levels of creative control. Now Capture Apple ProRAV Photos.

Mirror selfies (iOS 14.3) On all models, you can take a photo of the mirror that captures the image as you see it in the front camera. See Taking a Selfie.

Photos Filter photos into collections and albums and sort them by oldest or newest. Add the title to your pictures and videos so you can freely find them in Search. View Filter Photos in Albums, Sort Photos in Albums, and Add Descriptions, and View Photo and Video Details.

Measurement (iOS 14.1) On the iPhone 12 Pro and iPhone 12 Pro Max, you can instantly measure a person's height, use the ruler view to see individual measurement details, and use guides edge to more accurately measure flat edges, furniture, worktops, and more items.

Reminders-Reminders automatically suggest dates, times, and places for reminders based on similar reminders you have created in the past. You could also send reminders to people you share common lists with.

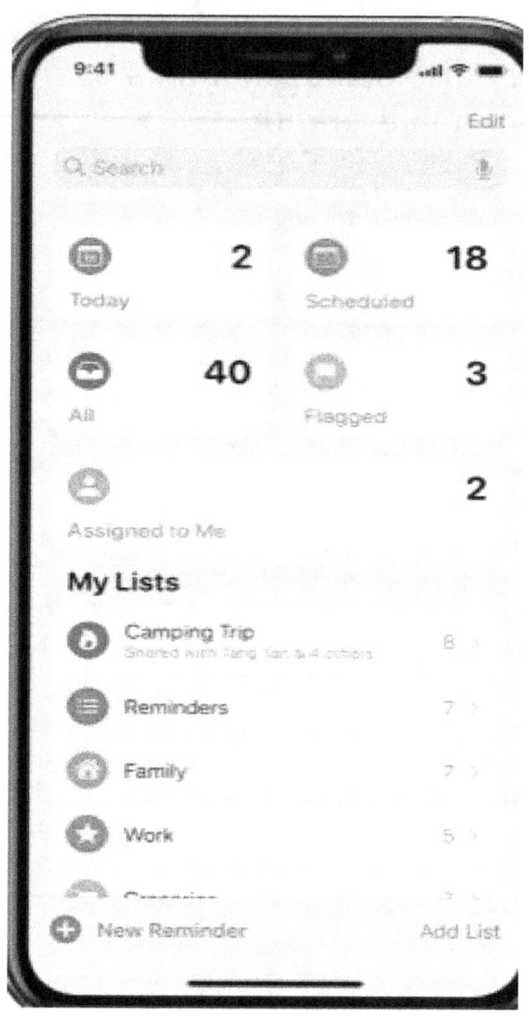

Siri-Siri has a new compact design that allows you to get information quickly while focusing on what you do. Siri now provides information from all over the web to help you find answers and you can send audio messages from the Messages app.

Safari- Safari is more secure and useful than ever. You can review the Privacy Report to understand how websites treat your privacy,

and Safari may tell you if the password you are using is unsafe. If you come across a website in another language, Safari now offers translations into seven different languages (beta). See View the Privacy Report and Translate the Web Page.

Health -A whole new sleep experience will help you reach your sleep goals and relax before bed.

You can use the Health Checklist to view and tune important features in the Health app. See Setting Up a Sleep Schedule and Managing Health Functions Through a Health Checklist.

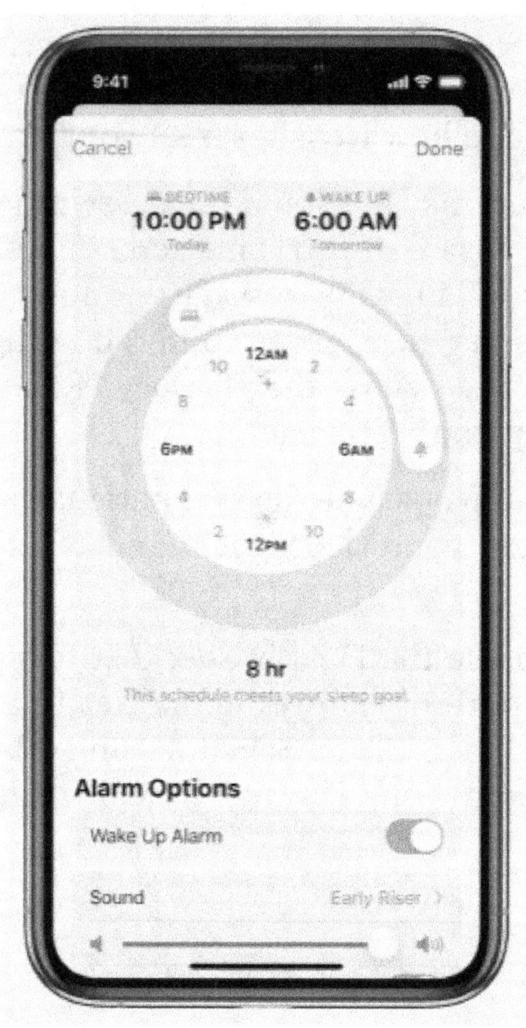

Cycle Factor Management (iOS 14.3) Helps manage health cycle monitoring predictions by recording factors such as pregnancy, breastfeeding, and contraceptive use.

Headphone volume -(iOS 14.2) Receive a notification and automatically reduce the volume of the headphones if the sound you hear is loud enough to affect your hearing.

You can also check the exact volume level as you play through your iPhone's ear and adjust the volume caps.

FaceTime -FaceTime can now identify when a participant is language signing and making a person different from the FaceTime group call.

Video calls are better natural, apart from the camera spot, makes you get eye contact when looking at the screen

Home-Adaptive home lighting allows you to change the temperature of the light during the day. Video cameras and doorbells can identify the people you've tagged in the Photos app, and you can be alerted when you move around in the activity zones you've set. See Turn on adjustable lighting, Adjust face recognition, and Organize rooms into zones.

Car Keys -Hold the car's digital key in the Wallet application so you can leave your car's physical keys at home. Simply bring the iPhone close to the car door to open it. When you enter, place your iPhone on a wireless reader or charger to start the car. You can also give keys to friends and family and personalized controls for another driver.

Car-Play- Choose from a range of well-featured wallpapers. CarPlay also supports new types of applications - parking, electric vehicle charging, and fast food ordering. See Change the background in CarPlay and Use other applications with CarPlay.

Privacy- The new setting allows you to share only the approximate location with the app, and the indicator appears at the top of the device screen whenever the app uses your camera or microphone.

App Store (iOS 14.3) You can now view apps' privacy practices before downloading them. The product page of each application shows a summary of the privacy protection reported by the developers, including the data collected.

Learn tricks for iOS 14 The Tips app often adds new tips so you can make the most of your iPhone.

Access Features from The iPhone Lock Screen

The lock screen will show the recent time and date and newest notifications when you wake up your device.

On the lock screen, you can see notifications, open the Camera and Control Center easily, and more.

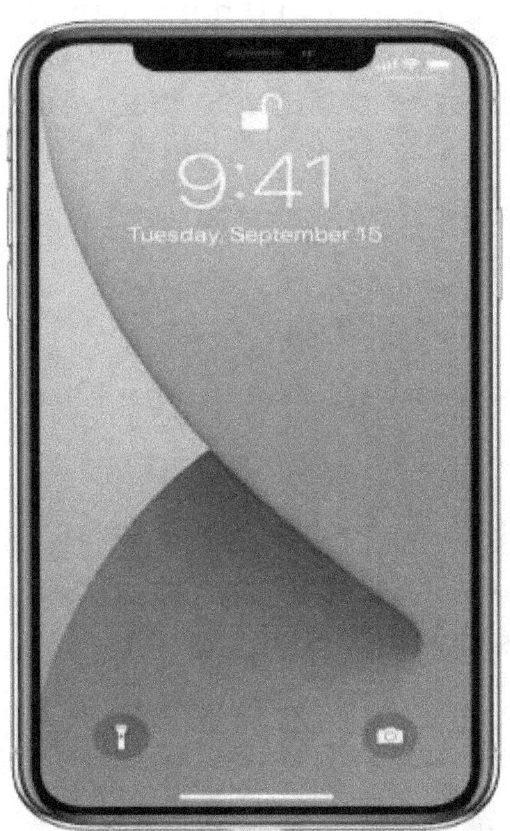

You can access useful features and information on the lock screen. On the lock screen, do one of the these:

-Open the camera: Swipe left. On supported models, you can touch and hold the Camera button, then remove your finger. (See Taking photos with an iPhone camera.)

-Open Control Center: Flip down from the top right corner (on an iPhone with Face ID) or jump over the bottom edge of the screen (on other iPhone models). (See Using and Customizing the Control Center on an iPhone.)

-See previous notifications: Swipe up from the center.

-See View Today: Swipe right

Display Notification On The Lock Screen

1.Go to Settings> Notifications.

2.Touch Show preview, then Always.

The notification includes text, lines on mail messages, an invitation on the calendar and more

Face Id And Passcode

Set the face ID

Before setting your Face ID, make sure there is nothing to cover the True Depth cameras or your face.

Face ID is make to work with glasses and contacts. You are unable to set a face ID if something disturbs you in your nose and mouth, like a face mask.

Face ID works best when your iPhone is approximately within arm's reach or closer (10-20 inches) to your face.

Set A Face Id

1.Go to Settings> Face ID and Password. Enter a password, if required.

2.Touch Set Face ID.

3.Hold the device in an upright position, place your face in front of the device, and tap Start.

4.Place your face in the frame and move your head slightly to complete the circle.

5.When you have finished scanning the form for the first time, tap Continue.

6.Gently move your head to complete the circle a second time.

7.Tap Done.

> If you did not set a password, you will need to create one for an alternate authentication method.
> To select the features, you want to use Face ID with or reset Face ID, go to Settings> Face ID and Password.

Temporarily disable Face ID

You can shortly stop Face ID from unlocking your device.

1.Press and hold the side key and any volume key for two seconds.

2.When the sliders appear, press the side button to lock the iPhone immediately.

✓ iPhone locks suddenly if you fail to touch the screen for a moment.
✓ The next time you unlock your iPhone with a password, Face ID will be enabled again.

Turn off Face ID

1.Go to Settings> Face ID and Password.

2.Do one of the following:

. Switch off Face ID only for some items: switch off one or more options, iPhone Unlock, Apple Pay, iTunes, or Safari AutoFill, and more.

. To turn off Face ID: Touch Reset Face ID.

NOTIFICATION

Review and respond to notifications on iPhone

Notifications help you keep up to date - let you know if you missed a call if the date of the event has moved, and more. You can adjust your notification settings so that you only see what's important to you. View notifications and respond to iPhone's lock screen or notification center.

Find all your notifications in one place

iPhone shows notifications immediately they arrive, but if you fail to read them at that moment, they're saving in the Notification Center so you can check them later.

To view notifications in the notification center, do one of the following:

. On the lock screen: Swipe or slide up from the center of the screen.

. On other screens: drag from top to middle. You can then scroll up to see any older notifications.

To close the Notification point, slide from the bottom up with one finger, or click the Home button.

Reply To Notifications

When you have multiple notifications in the notification center or on the lock screen, they are sorted by apps, making it easy to view and manage. You can also sort the notifications of some applications by organizing functions within the application, such as threads or threads. Merged notifications are displayed as small bundles, with the most recent notification at the top.

Do one of the following:

- ✓ To expand a group of notifications to view them individually, tap the group. To close it again, close show less.
- ✓ Click and drag a notification to see it and take quick actions if the app offers them (on supported models).
- ✓ Click the notification to open the app it comes from.

Discard, delete, and manage notifications

Do one of the following:

1. Process the notification you receive while using another app: drag it down to review it, then drag it up to discard it.

2. To delete a notification: Drag left over a notification or notification group and tap Delete or Delete all.

3. To send notifications directly to the notification center: Swipe left after a notification or notification group, tap Manage, and then tap Deliver silently. This prevents messages from this app or group from appearing on the lock screen, playing audio, illuminating the screen, or displaying stickers.

To view and hear these notifications again, swipe left after the notification in the notification center, tap Manage, and then tap Send.

I. To turn off notifications for an app or notification group: Swipe left after a notification or notification group, tap Manage, and then tap Turn off.

II. To change how notifications are displayed: Swipe left after the notification, tap Manage, tap Settings, and select an option. You can select whether to allow notifications alert on the app or not.

III. Delete all notifications in the notification center: Tap the Clear notifications button, then tap Delete.

If you didn't use the app for some time, Siri suggests switching off notifications for that app.

CHANGE ALERT STYLES

To add or change an alert style:

1.Go to Settings> Notifications.

2.In the Notification style section, select the application.

3.Select the type of warning and the style of the captions.

You can also turn sounds and tags on or off.

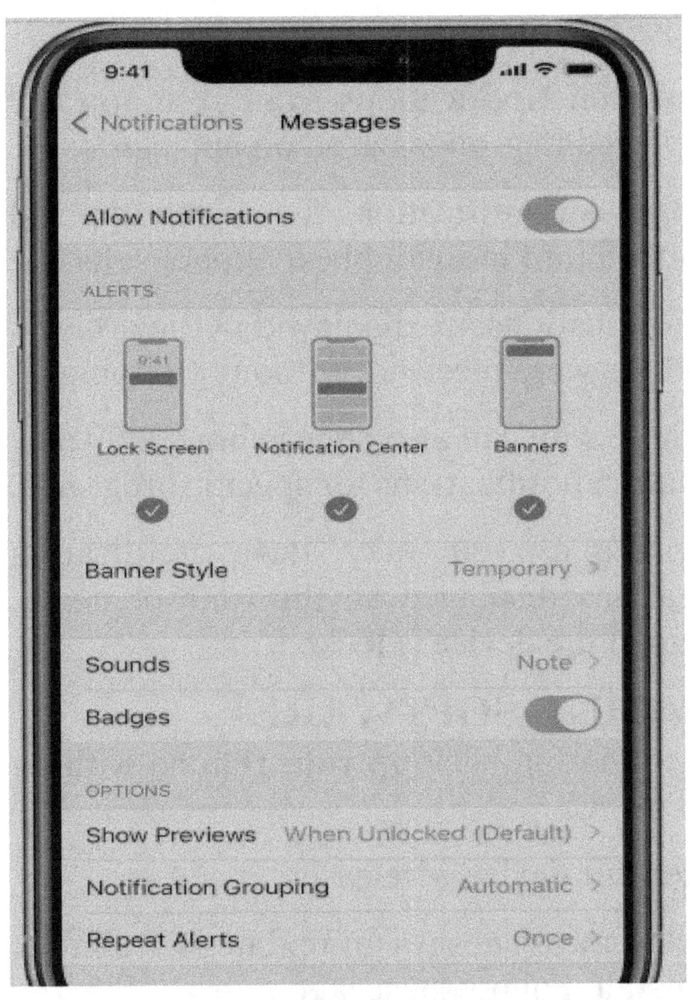

Change The Group Notification Settings

You can use notification alerts put together or separate them.

1.Go to Settings> Notifications.

2.Select an app and tap Group notifications.

3.Choose one of these options:

Automatic: Notifications from each app will be displayed in groups based on app alerts.

By apps: All notifications from each app will be grouped into individual expandable alerts.

Off: Notifications are displayed in the order in which they were received, without grouping.

From here, you can also choose how to display notification notifications for specific programs.

For example, you may have notification notifications displayed all the time or never, even when the device is locked.

UPDATING SOFTWARE

Before updating back up your iPhone with an iCloud or PC.

Update your device wirelessly

When the message says an update is available, click Install. Follow these steps:

1.Connect the device to the power supply and connect to the Internet via Wi-Fi.

2.Launch Settings> General and click Software Update.

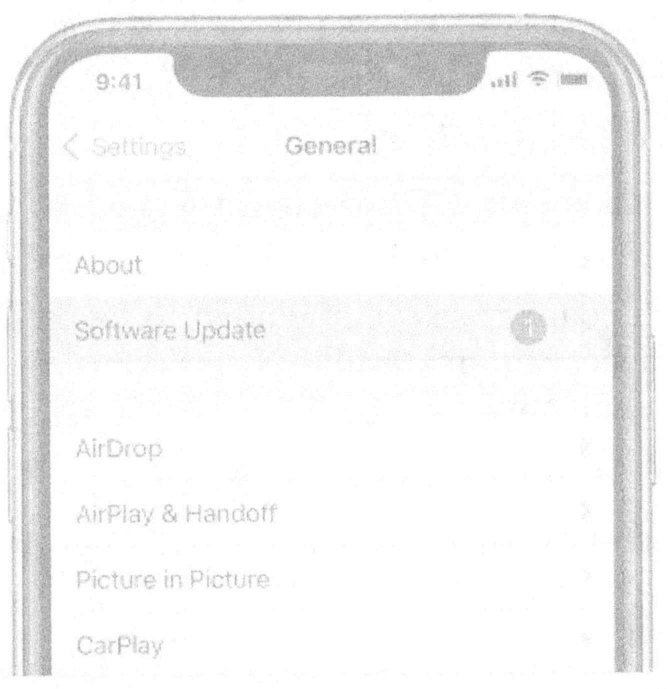

3.Touch Download and install. If the message asks you to temporarily uninstall programs because the software needs more space to update, tap Continue or Cancel. Later, iOS or iPadOS will reinstall the removed apps. If you tap Cancel, learn as much as you can.

4.To update immediately, tap Install. Alternatively, tap later and select Install Tonight or Remind Me Later. If you tap Install Tonight, just turn on the device before bed. The device will automatically update overnight.

5.Enter a password if required. If you don't know the password, learn what to do.

Update iOS to iPhone

When you update iOS to the latest version, your data and settings remain unchanged.

Before updating, set your iPhone to back up your device automatically or back up your device manually.

Update iPhone automatically

If you didn't turn on automatic updating the first time you set up your iPhone, do the following:

1.Go to Settings> General> Software Update.

2.Touch Customize automatic updates (or Automatic Updates). You can decide to download and install them automatically.

Connect your device to charge overnight as well as connect to Wi-Fi. So when the update is ready, the device downloads and installs the update. You will be told before installing the update.

Update your iPhone manually

You can search for and install software at any time.

Go to Settings> General> Software Update.

The screen displays the recently installed version of iOS and checks whether an update is available.

To switch off automatic update, launch Settings> General> Software Update> Automatic Update).

CHAPTER TWO

START TO USE YOUR iPhone

Steps to close apps on iPhone 12

1.Open the application you want to close.

2.You should see a long line at the end of the screen.

3.Hold this line with your finger and drag it up to close the app.

4.The iPhone 12 app should now be closed.

Closing multiple applications

1.Open the Home screen.

2.Place your finger on the bottom of the screen and slide it up.

3.You should now see all open apps in the background.

4.Slide each running application to close them.

NAVIGATE AROUND

Use gestures to navigate iPhone with Face ID

Use gestures with Face ID to easily swipe, do many tasks, change settings, and access all the things you do most often.

Learn the basics

Use the Side button to turn on iPhone, put it to sleep, use Siri, Apple Pay, and more.

On or off

- To switch it on, click and hold the edge button until the Apple logo appears.
- To switch it off, click and hold the side button and the volume button at the same time until the slider appears, and then drag to switch it off.

wakes up and sleeps

- Pick up to wake up, or tap to wake up iPhone.
- make a sleepy iPhone, press the side button.

Use Siri

Say Hello Siri or Press and hold the edge button.

Install the programs

After choosing an app in the App Store, quickly click twice on the Side knob to install it.

Use Apple Pay

To verify the authenticity of your purchases with Apple Pay with Face ID, double-click the Side button and view your iPhone.

Use intuitive gestures to navigate around

To create a continuous surface, the Home button has been replaced with new navigation modes.

Unlock and open the home screen

- To unlock iPhone with Face ID, take a look at iPhone, then drag it up from the bottom of the lock screen. However, if your iPhone is on a table or other flat surface, you can lift it or touch it to wake it up.
- To open the Home screen at any time, drag from the bottom edge of the screen.

Multitask

Slide up from the bottom screen and stop. When you are on the app, slide right with the edge bottom of the screen to switch to another app.

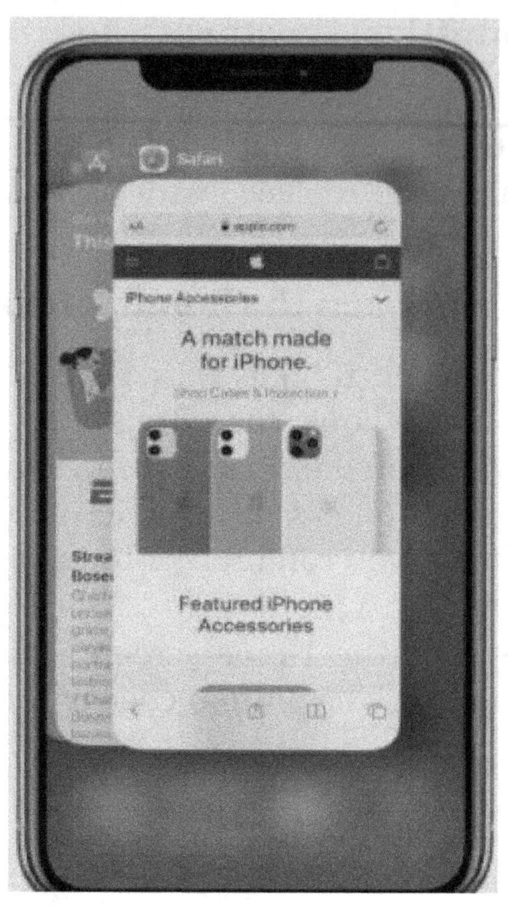

Find widget

To view data from apps you've added to gadgets, swipe right from the Home or Lock screen to open View Today.

You can also find gadgets on the Home screen if you've added them there.

SEARCH

To quickly find something on your device and online, swipe down from the center of the screen.

Open the Control Center

To quickly adjust settings and programs in Control Center, swipe down from the top right corner of the screen.

SIRI

Set Siri

If you didn't set Siri when you first set up iPhone, go to Settings> Siri & Search, and then do one of the following:

-If you want to call Siri with your voice: Turn on Listen to "Hey Siri".

-If you want to call Siri with the button: Switch on, click the edge button for Siri (on the device with Face ID) Touch Home for Siri (on the device with Home button).

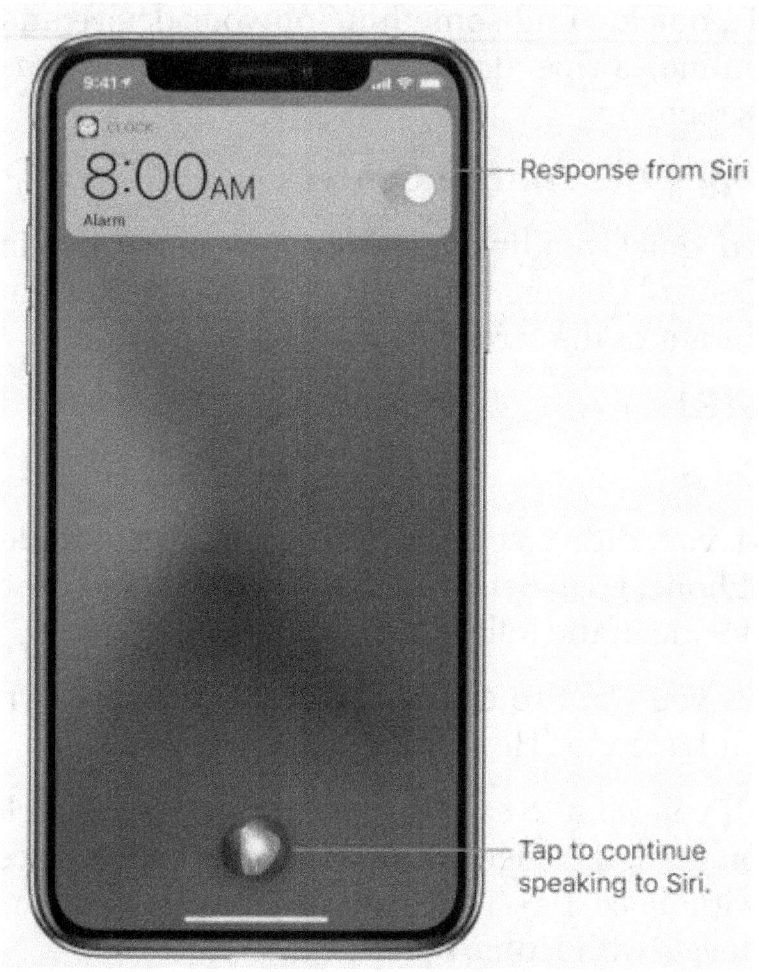

Call Siri with your voice

When you call Siri with your voice, Siri answers out loud.

1.Say Hello Siri and then question Siri.

For example, say something like Hello Siri, how is the weather like today? or Hi Siri, set the alarm to 11:30 in the morning."

2.To ask another question to Siri or perform another task, repeat "Hey Siri" or tap the Listen button.

Call the Siri button

When you press the Siri button, Siri responds loudly when the iPhone is in ring mode and quietly when the iPhone is in silent mode. See Changing the iPhone to Silent Mode. To change that, see Change the way Siri reacts.

1.Do one of the following:

- The device with Face ID: Click and hold the edge button.
- iPhone with the Home button: Click and hold the Home button.
- EarPods: Tap and hold the middle or call button.
- CarPlay: Tap and hold the voice command button on the steering wheel or touch and hold the Home button on the CarPlay home screen. (See Using Siri to Control CarPlay.)
- Siri Eyes Free: Press and hold the voice command button on the steering wheel.

2.When Siri shows, a question to Siri.

For example, say something like What's the 14.9 percent of 2500? Or Set the clock to 30 minutes.

3.To ask another question to Siri or perform another task, tap the Listen button.

You can also call Siri by tapping on the AirPods. See Using Siri with AirPods on your iPhone.

Correct if Siri misunderstands you

Reform your request: Tap the Listen button, and then say your request differently.

Say part of the request: Tap the Listen button, then repeat the request by saying words that Siri did not understand. For example, say "Call" and then enter the person's name.

Change the message before sending it: Say "Change".

Edit the request by text: If you see the request on the screen, you can edit it. Touch the request, then use the on-screen keyboard.

Type instead of talking to Siri

1.Go to Settings> Accessibility> Siri, then turn on Type for Siri.

2.To make a request, call Siri, then use the keyboard and text box to request Siri or do the task for you.

Tell Siri about yourself on your iPhone

If you tell Siri about yourself - including things like home address, work and relationships, like Send a message to Daughter and FaceTime Son.

Tell Siri who you are

1.Open Contacts, then fill in your contact information.

2.Launch Settings> Siri & Search> My Information, and then click your name.

Tell Siri how to pronounce your name

Say something like Hello Siri, learn to talk my name.

Tell Siri about the relationship

Say something like Hello Siri, Hope Joy is my wife, or Hello Siri, Suzanna is my mother.

Add Siri shortcuts to iPhone

Some apps offer shortcuts to things you do often, so you can ask Siri to do them for you. For example, a travel app might allow you to see an upcoming travel event simply by asking Siri, "Where do I go next?"

Add a suggested shortcut

Click add to Siri when you see a shortcut suggestion. And then follow the on-screen instructions to save the phrase of you want to start the shortcut.

You can also use the Shortcuts application to create a new shortcut using Siri or to manage, re-record, and delete existing Siri shortcuts. See the Shortcut User Guide.

Use a shortcut

Call Siri, then say a shortcut phrase.

About Siri suggestions on the iPhone

Siri makes suggestions for what you might want to do next, such as a meeting call or meeting confirmation, based on your routines and how to use the apps.

For example, Siri can help when you do one of the following:

Take a look at the lock screen or start your search: As Siri learns your routines, you get suggestions at the right time for exactly what you need.

Create emails and events: When you start adding people to an email event or calendar, Siri suggests people you've included in previous emails or events.

Receive a call: If you receive an incoming call from an unknown number, Siri will let you know who might be calling - based on the phone numbers included in your email.

Leave for the event: If your calendar event includes a location, Siri assesses the traffic situation and tells you when you need to leave.

View flight status: If you have a ticket to enter the post office or wallet, Siri displays your flight status in Maps. You can tap into the suggestion when you're ready to get directions to the airport.

Tips & Warnings As soon as you type, Siri can suggest movie names, locations - everything you've seen on an iPhone recently. If you tell a friend that you are on your way, Siri may even suggest your estimated time of arrival.

Safari Search: Siri suggests websites and other information in the search box while typing. On the keyboard, Siri also suggests words and phrases based on what you just read.

Confirm an appointment or book a flight on the travel website: Siri asks if you want to add it to your calendar.

Read the news: While Siri finds out what topics interest you, they are suggested in the News

Change The Way Siri Reacts

Go to Settings> Siri & Search, then do one of the following:

- Change voice for Siri: (not available in all languages) Touch Siri Voice, then select a male or female voice for Siri or change accent.
- Change when Siri gives voice answers: Tap Siri Answers, then select the option below Spoken answers.
- Always see the answer from Siri on the screen: Tap Siri Answers, then turn on Always Show Siri Captions.
- See your request on the screen: Tap Siri Answers, then turn on Always show speech.

NIGHT SHIFT

About the night shift

Night Shift1 uses the clock and geolocation of your device to determine when the sunset is in place. It then automatically switches the screen colors to warmer colors. In the morning, returns the screen to normal settings.

Turn on the night shift

There are two ways to turn the night shift on and off:

-Open the Control Center. Press the brightness control icon firmly, then tap the brightness icon to turn Night Shift on or off.

-Go to Settings> Display & Brightness> Night Shift. On the same screen, you can schedule the time to automatically turn on the night shift and adjust the color temperature.

Adjust the recording time

When shooting in night mode, a number appears next to the night mode icon to indicate how long the shot will last.

To do night mode photos, click the night mode button. Then use the slider above the shutter button to select Max, which extends the shooting time. When you take a photo, the slider becomes a countdown that counts down to the end of the shooting time.

Take self-portraits in night mode

1.Open the Camera app.

2.Touch the front camera button.

3.Keep your iPhone in front of you.

4.Take your selfie.

Record a slow night video

In low light conditions, you can use Time-lapse with nightstand mode by shooting movies at longer intervals.

Open the Camera app, then swipe left until you see Time-lapse. Touch the shutter button to record a video.

Use Night Mode Portrait

1.Open the Camera app and drag it in portrait mode.

2.Follow the on-screen tips.

3.Touch the shutter button.

SCREEN TIME

The time on the screen shows how you use your iPhone, including apps and websites you spend time with, how often you lift your device and more. With this information, you can decide how to manage the time spent on devices. You can set permissions and restrictions on the use of certain programs and websites, prevent access to explicit music and web content, and more.

Once you set the usage time, it starts compiling a description of how to use the device, including:

. How much time do you spend using apps by category (social networks, entertainment, reading, etc.)

. Analysis of the use of the application according to the time of day

. How much time do you spend on each application and which applications did you use within the deadline?

. See the types of notifications you receive and which apps send you the most notifications

. How often you start your device and what programs you use - this means how many times each program is used for the first time after downloading the device. You can tap each app in the screen time summary to see more information about how to use it.

Once the usage time is set, you can view the summary in Settings> Usage time> View all activities.

You can view a summary of device usage for the current day or last week.

Set The Usage Time On the iPhone

Over time, you can set permissions and restrictions on application usage, scheduled congestion, and more. You can switch off these settings at any time.

Set the downtime

You can block applications and notifications when you want the time away from the device.

1. Go to Settings> Screen Time.

2. Tap Turn on screen time, tap Continue and then tap This is my iPhone.

3. Touch Hibernation, and then turn Hibernation on.

4. Select Daily or change the days, then set the start and end times.

Set application limits

You can set a time limit for an application category (such as games or social networks) and individual programs.

1. Go to Settings> Screen Time.

2. If you haven't changed the screen time yet, click the screen time, click Continue, and then (This is my iPhone).

3. Touch Application Restrictions, and then touch Add Restriction.

4. Select one or more application categories.

To set restrictions for an individual program, click the category name to see all the programs in that group, and then select the programs you want to restrict. If you select multiple categories, the time limit applies to all.

5. Touch Next, and then set the time allowed.

To set the time for each day, tap Adjust days, then set limits for specific days.

6. To set a limit for multiple apps or categories, tap Select apps and repeat step 5.

7. When you have finished setting the limit, tap Add to return to the program restrictions screen.

To temporarily disable all application restrictions, on the Application Restrictions screen, touch Application Restrictions.

To temporarily turn off a category restriction, tap a category, then tap Application Restriction.

To remove a category restriction, tap a category, and then tap Restrict restriction.

Determine The Boundaries Of Communication

You can end some and outgoing calls or conversations, including FaceTime calls and messaging, at any time or at a specified time in your iCloud contacts.

1. If you haven't turned on your iCloud contacts yet, go to Set to [your iCloud name], and then turn on Contacts.

2. Go to Time Display Settings.

3. If you haven't changed the screen time yet, click the screen time, click Continue, and select my iPhone.

4. Touch Communication Restrictions and do one of the following:

. Restrict communication at any time:

tap Between screens then select Contacts only, Contacts and groups with at least one contact, or All.

To restrict communication during an interruption: tap During interruption. The option you selected during use is already set here. You can change this setting in individual contacts.

☐ If you select Specific contacts, tap Select from my contacts or Add a new contact to select the people you want to allow to communicate during the break.

☐ If a person who has recently been blocked by restriction settings tries to call or send you a message, their calls will not be successful.

If you make effort to call or send a message to someone who is recently blocked by communication restriction or limitation settings, their name or number will be displayed in red with an hourglass icon and communication will fail. If the restriction only applies to interruptions, you will receive a time-limited message. When the interruption is complete, you can resume communication with the contact.

☐ To continue communicating with blocked contacts using Restrict Communication Settings, change the settings in the above steps.

Select the programs you want to allow at any time

You may suddenly recognize the programs you want to use. Eg. In an emergency.

1. Open Time display settings.

2. Click Continue and select my iPhone.

3. Tap Always allowed, then tap or next to the app to add or remove it from the Allowed apps list.

SET UP A FAMILY SHARE ON THE IPHONE

Set up family sharing

Family Sharing requires (the organizer) to sign in with their Apple ID and verify the Apple ID you use for the iTunes Store, App Store, and Apple Books (you usually use the same Apple ID for everyone).

1. Go to Settings> [your name]> Family Sharing and follow the on-screen instructions to set up a group of family members.

. You can add family members or create a child account.

2. Touch the feature you want to share and follow the on-screen instructions.

. iCloud subscriptions and memory: You can share Apple subscriptions, iCloud storage plan, and subscriptions in the App Store.

. Purchases: You can share purchases with iTunes, App Store, Apple Books, and Apple TV. See Transferring Family Shopping.

. Locations: When you share your location with family members, they can use the Find My app to see your location and help find the missing device. See Sharing a location with family members and Finding the device of a missing family member.

. Kids Features: You can control your kids' spending and how they use Apple devices. See Include questions about buying children, setting up the Apple Cash family, and setting family sharing time.

You may need to set up a subscription, depending on the features you have selected. By choosing to share in-app purchases, music, movies, TV, and books with your family members, you agree to pay for all purchases that begin when they are part of a family group. Adult and teenage family members can independently opt-out of sharing purchases.

. **You can share photos, calendars, and more with family members.**

Add a family member

The family group organizer can add a family member.

1. Go to Settings> [your name]> Family Sharing and tap Add member.

2. Touch Invite person and follow the instructions on the screen.

You can send the invitation by AirDrop, SMS, or by mail. If you're close to a family member, you can also touch Invite in person and ask the family member to enter their Apple ID and password on a screen called "Apple Family ID."

Create an identity document for an apple for a child

An organizer, parent, or guardian can create an Apple ID for a child in a family group.

1. Launch Settings> your name> Family Sharing.

2. Do one of the following:

. If you are an organizer: tap Add member, tap Create an account for the child and follow the on-screen instructions.

. If you are a parent or guardian: tap Add a child and follow the on-screen instructions.

For more information about child accounts, see the article on Apple family sharing and Apple ID support for your child.

See what you share with your family

You can see what you're sharing with your family at any time, and adjust your sharing settings. Features you share with your family are displayed above the ones you didn't share.

1. Launch Settings> your name> Family Sharing.

2. Touch a feature and do one of the following:

. If you have not set the function: Follow the on-screen instructions to set it.

. If you have set the feature: View and adjust sharing settings.

A close family community

1. Go to Set to [your name] in Family Sharing for naming.

2. Do one of the following:

. Disband a family group: tap Stop using family. A group of families can only be dissolved by the organizer.

. To exit Family Sharing: tap Stop Family Sharing.

Young children cannot be removed from a family group and must be moved to another family before they become yours.

Download bulk purchases from the iTunes Store

1. Open the iTunes Store, tap More, and then tap Purchased.

2. Select a family member.

3. Touch a category (such as Music), tap the product you purchased, and then tap the Reload button to download it.

Download bulk purchases from the App Store

1. Open the App Store.

2. Touch the My Account - or profile picture in the upper right corner.

3. Tap Purchased, select a family member, and then tap the Reload button next to the purchased product to download it.

Download bulk purchases from Apple Books

1. Open the Books app.

2. In the upper right corner, tap the Account button or profile picture.

3. Touch the family member's name in the Family Purchases section and then the categories (for example, Books or Audiobooks).

4. Touch All, Recent Purchases, or Categories, then tap the Reload button next to the purchased product to download it.

Download bulk purchases from Apple TV

1. Open the Apple TV app.

2. Tap Library, tap Family sharing and then select a family member.

3. Touch a category (such as TV shows or movies) or category, tap the product you purchased, and then tap the Download button to download it.

How to stop sharing purchases with family members?

In addition to family sharing, the organizer can also include shopping sharing. All purchases made by family members are paid directly to the organizer's ID account.

If adults and children in the family do not want to share purchases and bills with family members, they can unsubscribe themselves.

Note: The family organizer could require that children in the family group get approval for purchase or free transfer.

1. Launch Settings> Your name> Family Sharing.

2. Touch Shopping Sharing, and then turn off Family Shopping Sharing.

If the organizer wants to completely turn off shopping sharing, they can touch the Stop Purchase Sharing option.

Switch on kids purchase on iPhone

Once you have set up Family Sharing, the family organizer may ask the children in the family group for permission to purchase or download for free. The purchase can be approved by the organizer or a parent or guardian in the family group.

1. Launch Settings> Your name> Family Sharing.

2. Touch Purchase Request, and then do one of the following:

. If there is no child in your family group: tap Add child or Create a child account and follow the on-screen instructions.

. If the child is in your family group: tap the child's name and then turn on Ask to Buy.

Set Apple Cash for Family (the US only)

For family sharing, the coordinator for children in family groups can set up an Apple wallet and then use the app to check the balance on the card. Besides, you can monitor transactions and reduce to whom the child can send money.

1. Launch Settings> Your name> Family Sharing.

2. Touch Apple Cash and do one of the following:

. If there is no child in your family group: tap Add child or Create a child account and follow the on-screen instructions.

. If there are children in your family group: Tap the child's name, tap Set Up Apple Cash, and follow the onscreen instructions.

Share subscriptions in the App Store

You can subscribe to the App Store, which you agree to share with family members.

For information about the App Store, see Download apps from the App Store for iPhone.

1. Launch Settings> your name> Subscriptions.

2. Do one of the following:

. Share all new subscriptions: Turn on sharing of recent subscriptions. When you buy a new subscription that is suitable for sharing, you share it with your family by default.

. To change specific subscription settings: Tap a subscription, and then turn Family Sharing on or off.

If you don't see the Family Sharing option, your subscription doesn't qualify for sharing.

To see which subscriptions you're sharing, go to [Your Name] Settings next to Family Sharing

Share your location with family members

As a family share, you can join the sharing of your area with family members. If the family director determines the area in the family sharing settings, the coordinator position is usually shared with everyone in the family. Families can then choose whether to share their place or not.

When you share your location with others, family members can see it in the Find Me menu, and if you lose it, they can help you find it. You can also be notified when family members change - for example if a child leaves school during school.

Note: To share your location, you need to turn on location services in Settings> Privacy.

1. Go to Settings> [your name]> Family Sharing> Location Sharing and turn on My Location Sharing.

2. If your iPhone doesn't currently share your location, tap Use this iPhone as my location.

3. Tap the name of the family member you want to share your location with, then tap Share my location.

You can repeat this step for each family member with whom you want to share your location. Each family member receives a message to share their place and can share their place with you.

4. To stop sharing your location with a family member, tap the family member's name and then Stop sharing my location.

You can use your location while using Mail. Click the profile picture or family member's name at the top of the conversation, tap the Information button, and then click Send my current location or Share my location.

Sharing a personal Hotspot

With Family Sharing, you can share your Internet connection through a personal access point with members of your family group. Once a member of your family group sets up a personal access point, other family members can use it without having to enter a password.

Set up your iPhone for a family member to find it

A family member can help you find the missing iPhone by doing the following on your device before you lose it:

. **Switch on-location services:** Go to Privacy Settings, and then turn on-location services.

. **Switch on Find My Device**: Launch Settings on your name to find my iPhone, and then switch on Find My iPhone and Send Last Location.

To set up other devices, see Add a device to find me on iPhone.

. To share a location with family members: Go to Settings> [your name]> Family sharing> Location sharing, and turn on Location sharing.

FIND THE DEVICE OF A FAMILY MEMBER

See Find your device in the Find me on iPhone section.

Devices are at the top of the list, and family members' devices are below yours.

CHAPTER THREE

iCloud

What is iCloud

iCloud securely saves photos, videos, files, music, apps, and more and keeps them up to date on all your devices. With iCloud, you can easily share photos, places, and more with friends and family.

iCloud can help you find your device if you lose it.

iCloud Photos securely save all your pictures and videos. And keeps them running on iOS devices, and iCloud.com. Any changes you make to the Photos app are updated anywhere automatically.

And with Shared Albums, it's easy to share photos and videos with the people you select and invite them to add photos, videos, and comments to your shared albums.

Sign in with your Apple ID

If you did not log in during setup, do the following:

1.Go to Settings.

2.ap Sign-on iPhone.

3.Enter your Apple ID and password.

If you don't have an Apple ID, you can do so.

4.If you are securing your account with two-step verification, enter a six-digit verification code.

If you have forgotten your Apple ID or password, see the Apple ID Recovery website.

Change your Apple ID settings

1.Go to Settings> [your name].

2.Do one of the following:

. Update your contact information

. Change your password

. Manage family sharing

Ways to Use iCloud on an iPhone

Update the following content regularly:

Messages, mail, contacts, calendars, notes, and reminders

Photos and videos

Music, apps, and books

Documents, see Setting up an iCloud Drive on an iPhone

Bookmarks, a reading list and web pages that open in Safari; see Browse the web using Safari on iPhone

Passwords and credit cards

You can also:

View your iCloud data on iPhone and iCloud.com (using a Mac or Windows PC).

Photos and videos should be shared with the persons you selected.

Share your iCloud storage on plans with 200GB or more for up to five other family members.

Find the missing iPhone, iPad, iPod touch, Apple Watch, Mac, or AirPods that you or your family members are missing. See Find a device in Sibni on an iPhone.

Find your friends and family; you, your friends, and family can share places, follow each other and see everyone's location on a map.

Back-Up and Restore Your Data

You can share an iCloud storage plan with five family members.

Ensure everyone in your family has a large iCloud space. Your family can share a single 200GB or 2TB storage plan for enough space for everyone.

When you share a storage plan, your photos and documents remain private and everyone continues to use their iCloud accounts - just like when you have your storage plan. Simply share the available space in the iCloud storage plan with family members, so you only have one management plan.

Share your storage plan with your existing family

On iPhone

1.Go to Settings> [your name].

2.Touch the Family Sharing.

3.Touch iCloud Storage.

4.Follow the steps to share an existing plan or, if necessary, upgrade to a 200GB or 2TB plan.

5.Use Messages to inform family members of an existing paid store plan that they can now switch to your shared store plan.

On your Mac

1.If necessary, upgrade to a 200 GB or 2 TB storage plan.

2.Select Apple > System Preferences and then click Family Sharing.

3.Click on iCloud Storage.

4.Click Share.

5.Follow the on-screen instructions.

macOS Mojave or earlier:

1.Select Apple menu> System Preferences and then touch iCloud.

2.Click Family Management.

3.Go to My Applications and Services.

4.Select iCloud Storage.

5.Click Start Sharing.

6.Click Done.

Set up recent family sharing and share a storage plan

Not using Family Sharing yet? Not a problem. You can share your iCloud repository when you first set up Family Sharing.

On iPhone

1.Go to Settings> [your name].

2.Tap Set family sharing and then tap Start.

3.Choose iCloud Storage as the first feature you want to share with your family.

4.If necessary, upgrade to a 200 GB or 2 TB storage plan.

5.When prompted, use Messages to invite up to five additional people to join your family and share a storage plan.

On Mac

1.Select Apple > System Preferences and then click Family Sharing.

2.Click on iCloud Storage.

3.Click Share.

macOS Mojave or earlier:

1.Select Apple menu> System Preferences and then press iCloud.

2.Click Manage on the down right edge.

3.Click on Change Storage Plan.

4.Upgrade to a 200 GB or 2 TB storage plan.

5.Go back to your iCloud settings and click Set Family. Follow the on-screen instructions.

6.When you're done, go to the My Applications and Services tab and select iCloud Storage.

7.Click Start Sharing

iCloud DRIVE AND FILES APP

Set up iCloud Drive on iPhone

Use the Files application to store files and folders in iCloud Drive. You can access them from any device you have signed in with the same Apple ID. Any changes you make appear on all your devices configured with iCloud Drive.

Turn on iCloud Drive

Launch Settings> Your name> iCloud, and then switch on iCloud Drive.

Choose which apps use iCloud Drive

Launch Settings> your name> iCloud, then turn on or off each of the apps listed in iCloud Drive.

Browse the iCloud Drive

1.Click browse at the bottom of the screen.

2.Under Location, tap iCloud Drive.

If you don't see Locations, retry Browse. If you don't see iCloud Drive in the Locations section, tap Locations.

3.To open a folder, click it

Search files and folders in Files

In the Files application, view and open documents, pictures, and other files.

View recently opened files

Tap Recently at the bottom of the screen.

Browse and open files and folders

1.Tap Search at the bottom of the screen and then tap an item on the Browses screen.

Click Browse again if you don't see it

2.Click to open file, location, or folder.

Note: If you did not install the application that created the file, open a quick preview of the file in the Quick Look file.

Find a specific file or folder

Enter a file name, folder name, or document type in the search box.

When searching, you have the following options:

-Focus on the scope of your search: Under the search box, tap Recently or the location or name of the tag.

-Start a new search: Tap the Clear text button in the search box.

-Open result: Touch it.

Go to list view or icon view

From an open location or directory, scroll down from the center of the screen, and then tap the View List button.

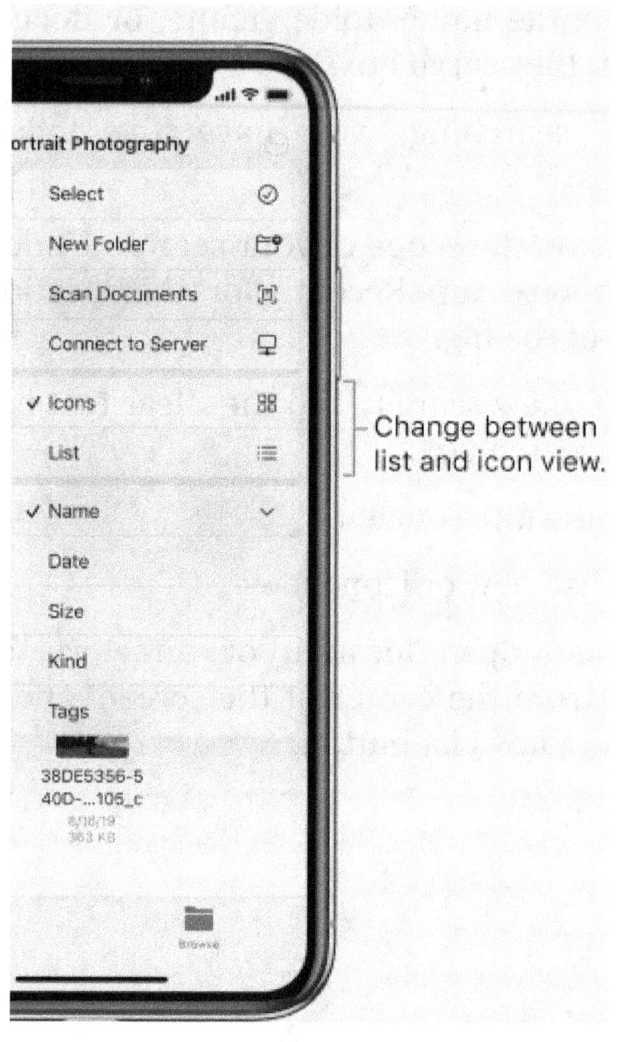

Change between list and icon view.

Change the way files and directories are selected

1.From an open location or directory, scroll down from the center of the screen.

2.Touch Sorted by and then select an option: Name, Date, Size, Type, or Labels.

Rearrange the Browse screen

Tap the More button at the top of the Browse screen, tap Edit, and then do one of the following:

-Hide location: Turn off location.

-Delete the bookmark and remove it from all items: Tap the Remove button next to the bookmark. (See Tagging a file or folder.)

-To remove an item from the favorites list: Tap the Remove button next to the item. (See Marking a folder as a favorite.)

-Change the order of the item: Touch and hold the Rearrange button, then move it to a new position.

Organize Files And Folders Into Files On Iphone

In the Files app, organize documents, pictures, and other files into directories.

Create a folder

1.Open an existing location or folder.

2.Swipe down from the center of the screen, tap the More button, and then click New Folder.

Note: If you do not see the New Folder, you cannot create a folder in that location.

Rename, compress, and make other changes to the file or folder

- Click and hold a file or folder, and then select either: Copy, Delete, Compress, and more.
- To edit multiple files or folders at once, tap Select, tap your options, and then tap an option at the bottom of the screen.

Highlights A File Or Folder

1.Touch and hold a file or folder, tap Bookmarks, then tap one or more bookmarks.

2.Touch Done.

To find the marked items, tap Browse, then tap the item below Tags.

To remove a tag, tap it again.

Mark a folder as a favorite

- Touch and hold a folder, then tap Favorite.
- To find Favorites, tap Browse.

CHAPTER FOUR

CALLS AND CONTACTS

Get in touch

Tap the Add button.

Find a contact

-Tap the search box at the top of the contact list, then enter a name, address, phone number, or other contact information.

-You can also search for contacts using a browser (see Use iPhone to Search).

Share a contact

-Tap a contact, tap Share, and then select how to send the contact information.

-Contact sharing sends all information from the contact card.

Delete contact

1.On the contact card, and then click Edit.

2.Scroll down, then tap Delete contact.

Use other contact accounts on iPhone

You can include contacts from other accounts in the Contacts application.

Use your iCloud contacts

Go to Settings> [your name]> iCloud, and then switch on Contacts.

Use Google Contacts

1.Go to Settings> Contacts> Accounts, then tap Google.

2. Sign in to your account, and then switch on Contacts.

Add contacts from another account

1.Go to Settings> Contacts> Accounts, then tap Add account

2.Select an account, sign in, and turn on Contacts.

Access to the Microsoft Exchange Global Address List

1.Go to Settings> Contacts> Accounts, then tap Exchange.

2.Log into your Exchange account, then turn on Contacts.

Set up a CardDAV account to able access school directories or business.

1.Launch Settings> Contacts> Accounts> Add Account, and then click Other.

2.Touch Add LDAP Account or Add CardDAV Account, then enter your account information.

Update your contacts regularly on all devices

1.You can use iCloud to regularly update your contact information on all your devices that are signed with the same Apple ID.

2.Go to Settings> [your name]> iCloud, then turn on Contacts.

Import contacts from SIM card (GSM)

Go to Settings> Contacts> Import SIM Contacts.

Import contacts from vCard

Tap the .vcf attachment in the email or message.

Add a contact from the directory

1.Click Groups and then tap the CardDAV directory you want to find.

2.Tap Done, then enter your search.

3.Touch a person's name to save their contact information.

Show or hide the group

- Tap Groups, then select the groups you want to view.
- This button only appears if you have multiple contact sources

MAKING CALLS

Call the iPhone

Dial the number on the keypad, click it, or select a number from the contact list.

Call the number

Ask Siri. Say call or call and then the number. Say each number differently - for example, four, two, six, six, seven, seven... You could say eight hundred for the 800 area code in the United States. Learn how to ask Siri.

Or do the following:

1.Touch the keyboard.

2.Do one of the following:

-Use the second line: On models with a Dual SIM card, tap the line at the top, and then select the line.

-Enter the number using the keypad: If you make a mistake, tap the Delete button.

-The last number again: Touch the Call button to see the last number dialed, and then touch the Call button to call that number.

-Type the number you copied: Tap the phone number box on the keypad, then tap Paste.

-Enter a soft pause (2 seconds): Touch and hold the star key (*) until a comma appears.

-Insert a hard pause (to stop dialing until you touch the dial button): Touch and hold the pound (#) button until a semicolon appears.

-Enter "+" for international calls: Touch and hold "o" until "+" appears.

3.Touch the Call button to start the call.

4.To end the call, tap the End button.

Invite your favorites

1.Tap Favorites, then select one to make the call.

On dual SIM models, iPhone selects the call line in the following order:

. The selected line for the contact (if set)

. The sim for the last call or from this contact

. Default voice line

2.To manage your favorites list, do one of the following:

. Add favorite: Tap the Add button, then select a contact.

. Rearrange or delete favorites: Tap Edit.

Redial or return a recent call

Ask Siri. Say something like call again the last number or return my last dial. You could:

1.Tap Recent, then select someone to make the call.

2.To get more information about the call and callers, tap the More Information button.

A red spot shows the number of calls missed.

Call someone from your contact list

Ask Siri. Say something like, Call Queen's cell phone. Learn how to ask Siri.

Or do the following:

1.In the Phone app, tap Contacts.

2.Tap a contact, then tap the phone number you want to call.

On models with Dual SIM cards, the default voice line is used for the call, unless you set the desired line for this contact.

Change the settings of the outgoing call

1.Go to Settings> Phone.

2.Do one of the following:

. Turn on Show Mi Caller ID: (GSM) Your phone number appears in Mi Number. For FaceTime calls, your phone number is displayed even if the caller ID is turned off.

. Turn on dial-up help for international calls: (GSM) When dial-up help is turned on, iPhone automatically adds the correct international or local prefix when calling contacts and favorites.

You can set up call transfer and call waiting on iPhone if you have a mobile service on the GSM network.

1.Go to Settings> Phone.

2.Touch any of the following:

-**Call transfer:** The call forwarding icon appears in the status bar when the call forwarding is turned on. You must be in the range of the mobile network when you set iPhone to send calls, otherwise, calls will not be sent.

-On models with a Dual SIM card, select a line.

-**Call waiting**: If you have a call and the call waiting is turned off, incoming calls go directly to your voicemail.

On Dual SIM models, call waiting for only works for incoming calls on the same line, unless Wi-Fi is activated on the other line and no data connection is available.

RECEIVING CALLS

Answer the call

Do one of the following:

1.Touch the Answer Call button.

2.If iPhone is locked, bring a slider.

Tips & Warnings You may have an iPhone that announces all incoming calls or incoming calls only while using a headset or Bluetooth in the car. Go to Settings> Phone> Call Announcement.

Put a call for silence

-Click the side button twice quickly

You can still answer the call quietly until you switch to voicemail.

Reject and send it to voicemail

Do one of the following:

1.Click the side button twice quickly.

2.Touch the Reject call button.

3.Swipe up on the call label.

You can also drop it on the call banner to see more options.

Do one of the following:

-Tap Remind me, then select when you want the reminder to return the call.

-Touch Message, then select Automatic reply or Tap Personalized.

To create your automatic replies, go to Settings> Phone> Reply with text, and then tap any default message and replace it with your text.

You may not be able to make or receive phone calls on iPhone if certain settings are turned on, if the software is outdated, or if there is a network problem.

Check iPhone settings

1.Turn airplane mode on and off.

Go to Settings and switch on Airplane Mode, stay for five seconds, then switch it off.

2.Check the Do Not Disturb settings. Go to Settings> Shake and make sure it's off.

3.Search for any phone number blocked. Go to Settings> Phone> Blocked Contacts.

4.See if call forwarding is turned on.

Go to Settings> Phone> Call Forwarding and ensure it switch off.

5.Make sure Silence Unknown Callers is turned on. If the setting is on, callers should be listed in your contacts or recent. They had to share their number in the mail or sent you a message using that number to forward the call. Add their number to Contacts to make sure the phone is ringing. Calls from some independent applications may not pass.

Update your software

1.Check for operator settings updates.

2.Check for iOS software updates. Some updates may require a Wi-Fi connection.

Remove and reinsert the SIM card

-If your iPhone has a SIM card, remove it, and then insert it again.

Contact your mobile operator

When contacting your mobile operator, be sure:

1.Your account is set up to use your iPhone.

2.There are no localized service interruptions.

3.Your account does not have an account-related block.

4.Your calls have no errors in the mobile operator's system.

Check the network settings

1.**Reset the network settings**. Launch Settings to General> Reset Network Settings. This erases all recently saved settings, including Wi-Fi passwords, preferred networks, and VPN settings.

2.Try making or receiving phone calls elsewhere.

-Switch to another network band. Go to Settings> Mobile> Mobile Data Options> Enable LTE and turn off Enable LTE, 4G, or 3G (this option depends on your mobile operator and your device model).

Setting Ringtone

Choose ringtones and vibrations on iPhone

You can set a default ringtone and assign distinctive ringtones to specific people. You can also use a vibrator and turn off the bell.

Change the warning and vibration tones

-See Replace iPhone sounds and vibrations.

-iPhone comes with ringtones to play for incoming calls. You can buy more ringtones in the iTunes Store.

Assign another ringtone to the contact

1.Open the Contacts application.

2.Select a contact, tap Edit, tap Ringtone, and then select a ringtone.

Turn the ringtone on or off

-Turn the Ring / Silent switch to turn the silent mode on or off. The alarm clocks continue to ring when the silent mode is on

CHAPTER FIVE

ABOUT KEYBOARD

Change the keyboard settings

The language of the keyboard also determines the language of the dictionary used to predict the text.

To adjust the keyboard settings:

1.Open an application that uses the keyboard, such as Messaging or Mail.

2.Touch and hold or.

3.Touch keyboard settings.

4.Then personalize your settings.

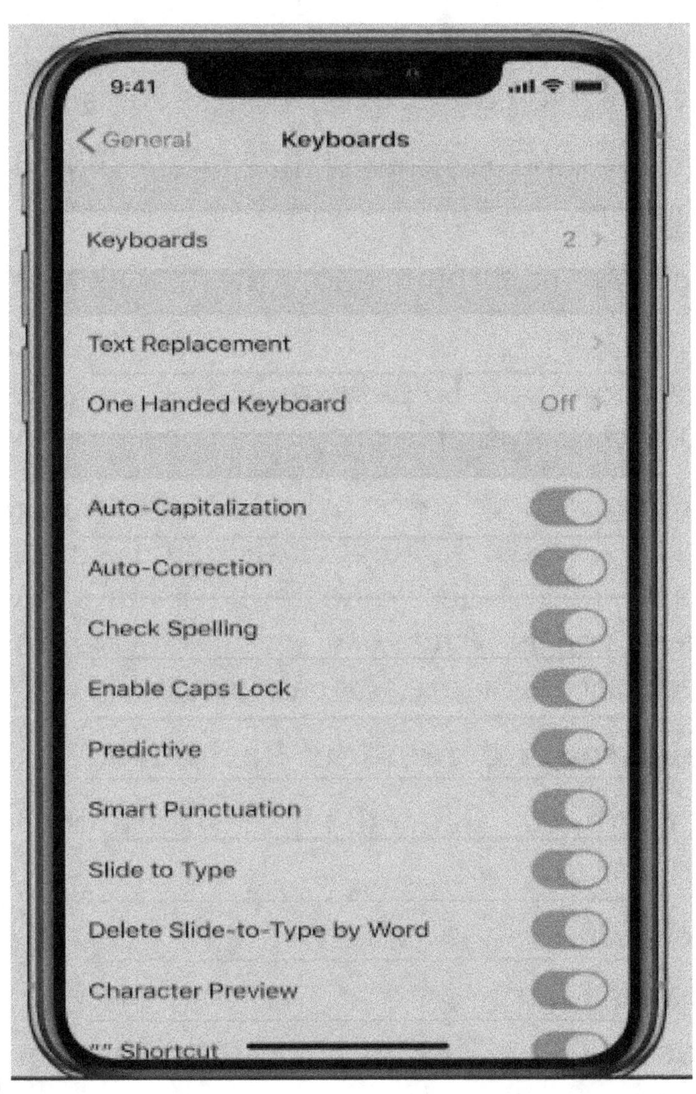

Add or erase a third-party keyboard application

You can install third-party keyboard applications as you install other applications on your device. After installing a new keyboard, add it before you can use it. Do these steps:

1.Go to the App Store and find the keyboard app you want.

2.Touch Get and then follow the installation instructions.

3.Enter your Apple ID password or use Face ID or Touch ID if available on your device.

4.Then add a new keyboard. Go to Settings> General> Keyboard> Keyboards> Add a new keyboard and select the application you installed. You may need to set the keypad to allow full access before you can use it.

To delete an independent keyboard:

1.Go to Settings> General, tap Keyboard, then tap Keyboard.

2.Touch Edit.

3.Tap, then tap Done.

You can also delete the keyboard by deleting the ancillary app you installed from the App Store.

Switch to another keyboard

While using the application, you can switch to another keyboard, such as a stand-alone keyboard or a language keyboard. Follow these steps:

1.Touch and hold or.

2.Select the keyboard you want to use.

To arrange keyboards:

1.Go to Settings> General> Keyboard and tap Keyboards.

2.Touch Edit.

3.Touch and hold three horizontal lines to move the keyboard.

4.Touch Done.

Third-party keyboards might not at times not accessible due to one of the following reasons:

-If the application developer you are using does not allow independent keyboards.

-If you type a secure text field, such as entering a password that shows characters typed as dots instead of letters and numbers.

-If you use the numeric keypad instead of the standard keyboard.

Instead, you see the default keyboard until you finish typing.

Change the physical keyboard layout

You can select from many keyboard layouts to match your physical keyboard keys. You can also use an alternative keyboard layout that does not match your physical keyboard keys.

To be able to change the physical keyboard, you need to compare it to an iPhone, iPad, or iPod touch. Follow the instructions that came with the keyboard to set it for detection or comparison mode. After connecting it, go to Settings> General> Hardware Keyboard, and select a schedule.

Learn how to set up and use Bluetooth accessories such as a keyboard with your device.

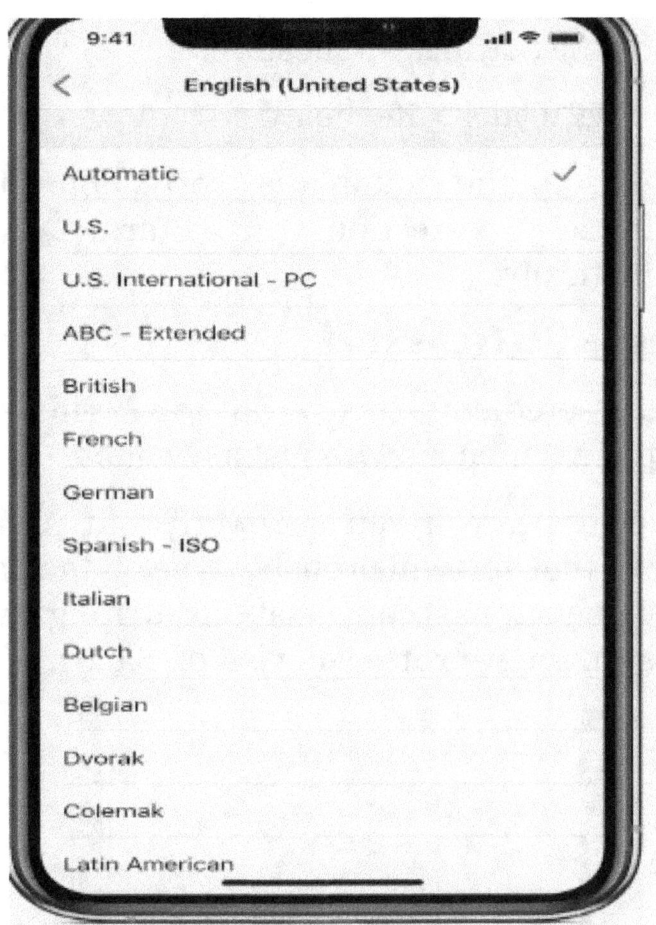

Use automatic correction

AutoCorrect uses the keyboard dictionary to check to spell while typing, it automatically corrects misspelled words for you. To use it, just insert a text box.

To make sure this setting is turned on, follow these steps:

1.Open the Settings application.

2.General Touch> Keyboard.

3.Turn on the automatic correction. The automatic correction is turned on automatically.

Use predictive text

With a predictive text, you can write and complete sentences with just a few taps

As you type, you can see word and phrase options that you will probably type on the back based on your past conversations, writing style, and even the websites you visit on Safari.

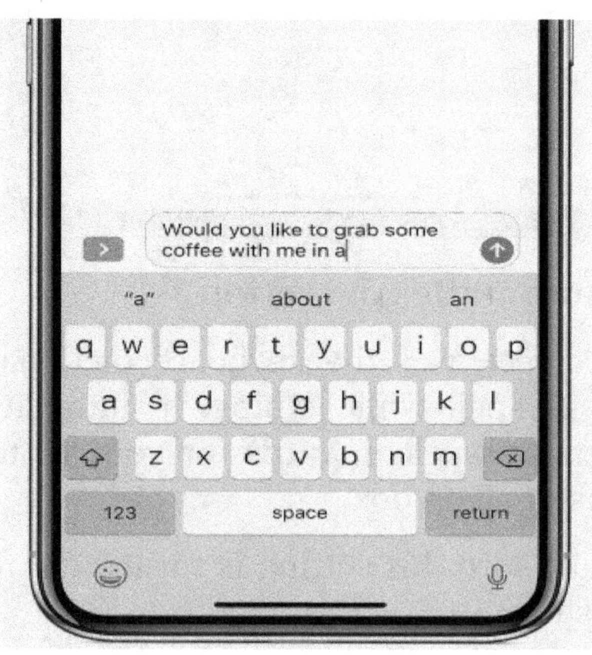

To turn on or off a predictive text, tap and hold an emoji icon or a globe icon. Touch keyboard settings, then turn on Prediction. Or go to Settings> General> Keyboard and turn the Predictive on or off.

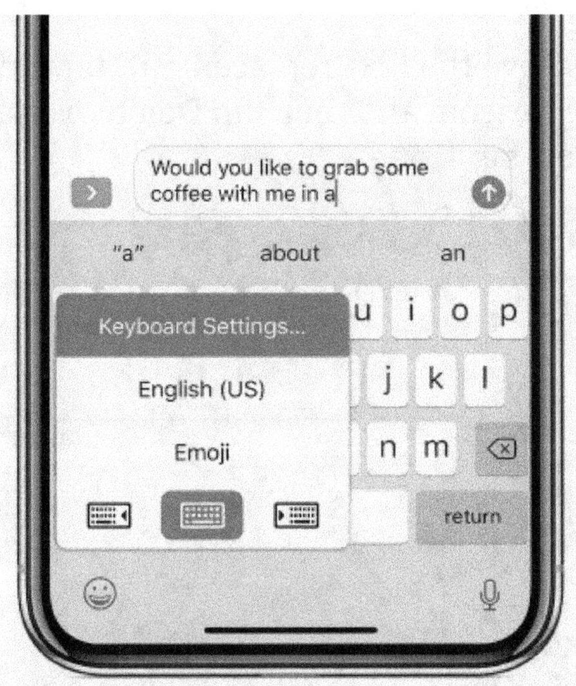

Set the text replacement

By replacing the text, you can use shortcuts to replace longer phrases. When you insert a shortcut into the text box, the phrase automatically replaces it. For example, you can enter "GM" and "Good Morning" to automatically change it.

To handle text replacement, tap Settings> General> Keyboard> Text Replacement.

-To add a substitute text, tap the plus icon, then enter a phrase and shortcut. When you are finished, tap Save.

-To remove the text replacement, tap Edit, tap the delete icon, and then tap Delete. To save the changes, tap Done.

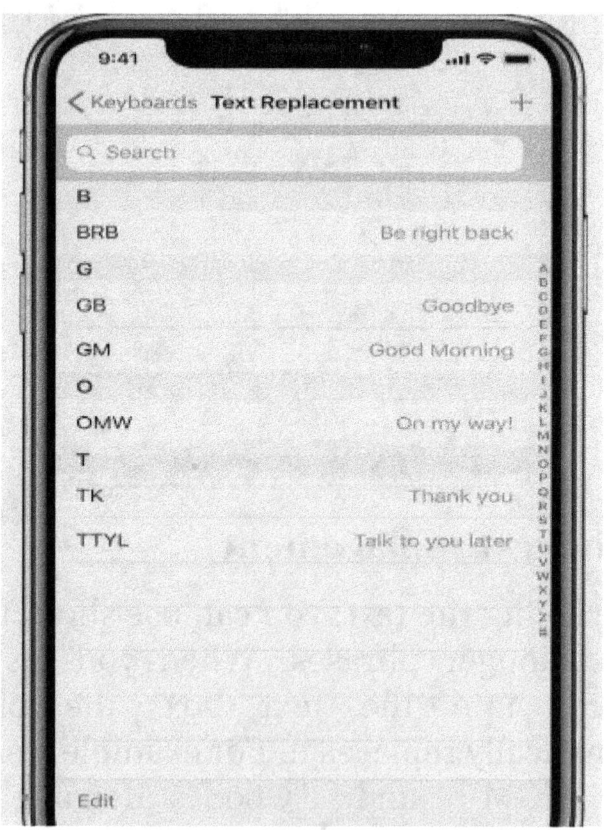

Text A Message

To send a text message to one or more persons.

1Tap the New Message button at the top of the screen to start a new message, or tap an existing message.

Message list, with the Edit button in the upper left corner and the Compose button in the upper right corner. The blue dot to the left of the message means unread.

2.Enter either the phone number, contact name, or ID of each receiver. Or click the Add button, then select contacts.

-On Dual SIM models, to send SMS / MMS from another line, tap the displayed line, then select another line. See also Managing Dual SIM Mobile Plans.

3.Tap the text box, type the message, and then tap the Send button to send.

-A warning icon appears if the message cannot be sent. Touch the alert to try sending the message again.

Tips & Warnings To see when a message has been sent or received, bring the message bubble to the left.

-To view the details of the conversation, tap a name or phone number at the top of the screen, then tap More Information. You can tap a contact to edit the contact card, share your location, view attachments, leave a group chat, and more.

-To return to the message list from the conversation, tap the Back button or move from the left edge.

Reply to the message

Ask Siri. Say something like:

. Send a message to Madam Rita saying a day after tomorrow

-Read my last message from Jackson

-Answer is good news.

Share Your Name And Photo

In the Messages app, you can share your name and photo when you start or reply to a new message. Your photo can be a Memoji or a custom image. When you open Messages for the first time, follow the instructions on the iPhone to select your name and photo.

To change the name, photo, or sharing options, open Messages, tap More options, tap Edit name and photo, and then do one of the following:

. Change the profile picture: Tap Edit, then select an option.

. Rename: Tap the text fields where your name appears.

. Turn to share on or off: Tap the button next to Sharing names and photos (green indicates it's on).

. Change who can see your profile: Tap the option under Auto Share (Names and photo sharing should be turned on).

The name and photo of your messages can also be used for your Apple ID and My Contacts Card.

Pick Up the Conversation

You can put certain conversations at the top of the message list so that the people you contact are always first on the list.

Do one of the following:

. Swipe right on the conversation, then tap the Pin button.

. Touch and hold a conversation, then bring it to the top of the list.

Disconnect the conversation

You can mark certain conversations at the top of the message list.

Do one of the following:

. Touch and hold the conversation, then drag the message to the bottom of the list.

. Touch and hold the conversation, then tap the Undo button.

Switch from a conversation in Messages to FaceTime or an audio call

In a Messaging conversation, you can start a FaceTime or audio call with the person you are chatting with within the Messages application.

1.In a message conversation, tap a picture or profile name at the top of the conversation.

2.Touch FaceTime or Audio.

How to Send Money in Messages Application?

When you send money in the Messages application using Apple Pay, your Apple Cash card is automatically used for the first payment. If you use a debit card instead, you can send money directly from your debit card.

Watch the demo to see how you can send money to your device or use the steps below.

On an iPhone

1.Open the Messages app, and then commence a new dialogue or click an existing one.

2.Tap the Apple Pay button on the Apple Pay icon. If you don't see the Apple Pay button, tap the App Store icon first.

3.Enter the amount you want to send.

4.Touch Pay, then tap the Send button of the Send icon to view or cancel your payment.

5.Confirm payment with Face ID, Touch ID, or password.

If the person who sent you the money has not yet accepted the money, you can cancel the payment.

Respond to a request for money

1.Open the request in the Messages app, then tap Pai on the message.

2.Review the amount you want to send. Touch Pay to continue or change the amount.

3.Confirm with Face ID, Touch ID, or password and send payment.

To reject a request for money, simply ignore the message

On your iPhone

1.Open a conversation in Messages or start a new conversation.

2.Tap the Apple Pai icon Apple Pai. If you don't see the Apple Pay button, first tap the App Store button on the App Store icon.

3.Enter the amount, then tap Request.

4.Submit your request.

How to Cancel Or Contest A Payment

1.Open the Messages app, and then open the dialogue and click the payment.

2.Your Apple Cash card opens in the Wallet app. Under Recent Transactions, tap the payment, then tap again.

3.Touch Cancel payment.

If you do not see Cancel payment, the person has already accepted payment. Try asking the recipient to return your money.

CHAPTER SIX

ONLINE WORLD

Connect your iPhone to the Internet using available Wi-Fi or a mobile network.

Connect your iPhone to the Wi-Fi network

1.Launch Settings> Wi-Fi and then switch on Wi-Fi.

2.Tap one of the following:

-**Network**: Enter a password, if required.

-**Other:** Joins a hidden network. Enter the hidden network name, security type, and password.

If the Wi-Fi icon shows at the top of the screen, the phone is connected to the Wi-Fi network. Your Phone reconnects when you return to the same location.

Join a personal hotspot

If your iPad (Wi-Fi + mobile) or other iPhone shares a personal access point, you can use its mobile internet connection.

Go to Settings> Wi-Fi, then select the device name that shares the Personal Access Point.

If prompted for a password on your iPhone, enter the password shown in Settings> Mobile> Personal Hotspot on the Personal Hotspot sharing device.

Connect iPhone to your mobile network

The iPhone automatically connects to your mobile operator's mobile data network if a Wi-Fi network is not available. If the iPhone does not connect, check the following:

1.Make sure the SIM card is activated and open. See Setting up a mobile service on an iPhone.

2.Go to Settings> Mobile.

3.Make sure the mobile data is turned on. On models with a Dual SIM card, tap Mobile Data, then confirm the selected line. (You can only select one mobile data line.

Browse websites with SAFARI

With a few taps, you can easily navigate the web page.

-**Return to top:** Twice click the top edge of the screen to easily return to the top page.

-See more pages: Rotate the iPhone horizontally.

-Refresh page: Tap the Reload button next to the address in the search box.

-Share links: Touch the Share button.

Change the text size, display, and website settings

Use the View menu to increase or reduce text size, switch to reader vision, define privacy limitation, and more.

Open the View menu, click the Website Options on the left side of the search box, and then do these:

-**Change the font size**: A major touch to increase the font size or a lowercase A to decrease it.

-Browse a web page without advertisements or navigation menus: Touch Show Reader (if available).

-Hide search box: Tap the Hide toolbar (tap the top of the screen to restore it).

-See PC website version: Touch Request desktop website (if available).

-Set the display and privacy controls every time you visit this website: Touch Web Settings.

Translate A Web Page

When you come across a website in another language, you can use Safari to translate text (beta; not available in all languages or regions).

-When viewing a webpage in another language, tap the Webpage Options button, and then tap Translate

Check the privacy and security settings for Safari

Go to Settings> Safari, then under Privacy and Security turn on or off any of the following:

Prevent multiple location tracking: Safari restricts third-party cookies and data automatically. Disable this option to allow tracking of multiple locations.

Block all cookies: Make this option to prevent websites from adding cookies to your iPhone. (To remove cookies that are already on iPhone, go to Settings> Safari> Clean History and Data Website)

Fraudulent website alert: Safari displays a warning if you visit a suspicious phishing website. Disable this option if you do not want to be warned about fake websites.

Check Apple Pay: Websites that use Apple Pay can check to see if Apple Pay is enabled on your device. Turn off this option to prevent websites from checking to see if you have an Apple Pay.

When you visit a website that uses unsafe Safari, a warning appears in the Safari search box.

Clear browsing history and data

Launch Settings> Safari> Clean History and Data Website

Set up an E-mail account

1.Go to Settings> Mail> Accounts> Add Account.

Do one of the following:

. Tap an email service - for example, iCloud or Microsoft Exchange - and then enter your email account information.

. Tap Other, tap Add email account and then enter your information to set up a new account.

How to set up an email account automatically

If you use iCloud, or Yahoo, you can set up your email account and password. See how:

1.Go to Settings> Mail, then tap Accounts.

2.Click add account and then select your email provider.

3.Enter your email address and password.

4.Click Next and wait for Mail to confirm your account.

5.Select information from your email accounts, such as Contacts or Calendars.

6.Touch Save

Manage email by swiping

While viewing your email list, you can simply crawl and drop individual email addresses, mark them as read, and more.

-To find a list of actions, flip the email to the left until you see a menu, then tap. To use the right action, quickly turn to the left.

-Swipe right to reveal another action.

-To select the actions you wish to show in the menus, launch Settings> Mail> Drag Options.

Organize Mail with Mailboxes

In the mailbox list, you can view all mailboxes, create a new one, or replace or delete it. (Some mailboxes cannot be changed.)

1.Click the Mailboxes in the upper left corner.

2.Click Edit at the top of the list.

3.Check the boxes next to the mailbox you want to view.

There are several smart mailboxes, such as Unread, that display email from all your accounts. Touch the mailboxes you want to view.

4.To add a mailbox, click the new mailbox at the down of the list.

5.Enter a name and define an area and then click Save.

Change the order of the mailboxes

You can reorganize your mailboxes so that the frequently use one will show at the top of your mailbox.

1.Tap the Mailboxes in the upper left corner.

2.Click edit at the top.

3.Touch and hold the Rearrange button next to the mailbox until it appears, and then bring it to the desired location.

Run or tick multiple emails

1.While viewing the list of email addresses, tap Edit.

2.Mark the email addresses you want to move to or tap their checkboxes.

To quickly select multiple email addresses, flip down from the checkboxes.

3.Select the action you want to perform on all selected emails.

If you change your mind, turn immediately to the left with three fingers to cancel.

View sketches of email addresses from all accounts

If you have many email accounts, you can see drafts from all accounts.

1.Click the Mailboxes in the upper left corner.

2.Click edit at the top of the list.

3.Click to add a mailbox, then turn on All Drafts mailbox.

Add Receivers

1.Tap the to the field, then type in the recipient's names.

As you type, Mail suggests a person's from your contacts, with their email addresses for those who have more than one email.

You can also tap the Add Contact button to open Contacts and add recipients from there.

2.If you are sending a copy, tap the Cc / Bcc field.

3.Tap in the Copy field, then enter the names of the people you are sending the copy to.

4.Tap in the Bcc field, then enter the names of people whose names you don't want to see other recipients.

Tips & Warnings After entering recipients, you can change the order of their names in the address fields or drag them from one field to another - for example, to the Bcc field if you choose not to have their name displayed.

Send A Copy To Yourself Automatically

-Go to Settings> Mail, then turn on Bcc Myself.

Add additional mail orders

1.Go to Settings> Mail> Accounts> Add Account, then tap Other.

2.Touch Add Email Account.

3.Enter your name, email, and password, and then click next.

4.Enter the names of the coming mails and outgoing ones, and server for your account with other required information.

5Touch Save.

Customize your email signature

You can customize the email signature that appears automatically at the bottom of each email you send.

1.Go to Settings> Mail, then tap Signature.

2.Tap in the text box at the top of the screen, then edit your signature.

Tips & Warnings If you have multiple email accounts, tap Using an account to set a different signature for each account.

Send An Email From Another Account

If you have multiple email accounts, you can specify from which account to send the email.

-Touch the From field to select an account.

Mark addresses outside specific fields

When you send an email to a recipient who is not in your organization's domain, the recipient's name may appear in red to tell you.

1.Go to Settings> Mail> Mark Addresses.

2.Insert areas in your organization - the ones you don't want to be marked in red.

You can enter domain domains separated by commas (for example, "apple.com, ekample.org").

Any emails sent to or from other domains are flagged.

CHAPTER SEVEN

ABOUT APPS

What is App

A software application developed for use on Apple's iOS-powered iPhones. iPhone applications are available through the Apple App Store and are designed to work on Apple's iOS mobile operating system, which runs the iPhone, as well as the iPad and iPod Touch devices.

What is App Store

Generally, an app store is an application that allows a user to find software and install it on his computer or mobile device.

It is a collection of free and commercial software, approved for use on your device.

You can view, purchase, download, install and update the software through the app store on your device.

How to pre-Install App

1.Before you begin

You may need an Apple ID password before downloading and installing applications on your iPhone.

2.Select the App Store

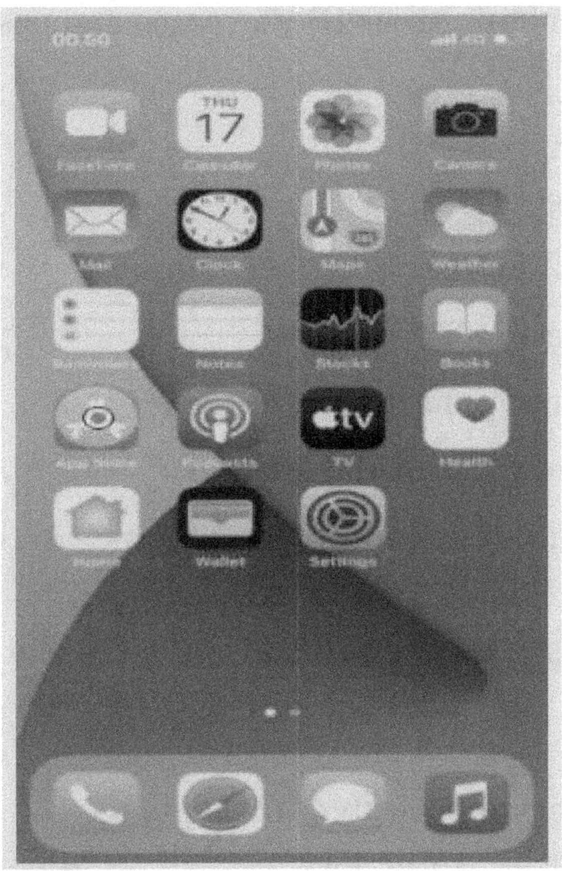

3.Select Search

4.Select the search bar

5.Enter the name of the application and select the search

6.Choose GET

Scroll down to find more search results.

7.Select Use an existing Apple ID

8.Enter your Apple ID username and password and select OK

9.Select Install

10. Select Done

11. Wait for the process to complete

12. Select OPEN

13. Your application is ready to use

Buy and Download the App

1.To purchase the app, tap the price. If the app is free, tap Download.

If you see the Download button instead of the price, you have already purchased the application and can download it for free.

2.If necessary, verify your Apple ID with a Face ID, Touch ID, or password to complete your purchase.

While the application is being downloaded, an icon with a progress indicator appears on the home screen. You can also find the application in the application library, in the Recently Added category.

Share an Application

1.Tap the app to see its details.

2.Tap the Share button, then select a share option or tap the Gift app (not available for all apps).

Receive or send a gift card to the App Store and iTunes

1.Tap the My Account button or a profile picture in the top right corner.

2.Tap one of the following:

. Use a gift or code

. Send the gift card by email

Subscribe To Apple Arcade

1.In the App Store, click Arcade, and then do one of the these:

. Start a free one-month subscription (if eligible): Try for free.

. Start a monthly subscription: Tap Subscribe.

2.Review your subscription details, then confirm with your Face ID, Touch ID, or Apple ID.

Unsubscribe from Apple Arcade

1.In the App Store, tap the My Account button or profile picture in the top right corner and then tap Subscriptions.

2.Touch Apple Arcade, then Unsubscribe.

After unsubscribing, you will unable to play any Apple Arcade games, even after download to your device.

Delete applications if you no longer need them

Update applications manually

On the iPhone and iPad, the applications you download from the App Store will be automatically updated. But if there is a problem, you can update the application manually.

How to Update Applications Manually on iPhone?

1.Open the App Store.

2.Tap the profile icon at the top of the screen.

3.Slide to see pending updates.

4.Press Update next to an app install the app only or click Update all.

Managing Your App

In the App Store, you can manage subscriptions and view and download purchases made by you or other family members.

You can also set limits and adjust your App Store settings in Settings

Approve Purchases Using Family Sharing

When Family Sharing is set, the family organizer can review and approve purchases made by other family members under a certain age.

Find and download applications purchased by you or family members

1.Tap the My Account button or a profile picture in the top right corner, then tap Purchased.

2.If you have set up Family Sharing, tap My Purchases or select a family member to view their purchases.

Note: Purchases made by family members can only be seen if they decide to share them. Purchases made through Family Sharing may not be available after a family member leaves the family group.

3.Find the app you want to download (if it's still available in the App Store), then tap the Download button.

Manage Your Subscriptions

1.Tap the My Account button or a profile picture in the top right corner, then tap Subscriptions.

2.Select a subscription, and then do one of the following:

-Replace or cancel an existing subscription.

-Subscribe to an expired subscription.

-Share your eligible App Store subscription with other family members in the family sharing group.

Change the App Store settings

Go to Settings> App Store, then do one of the following:

-Automatically download purchased applications on another Apple device: Under Applications automatically, turn on Applications below.

-Update applications automatically: Turn on app updates.

-Control the use of mobile data for application downloads: To allow downloads to use mobile data, turn on Automatic Download (under Mobile Data). To choose whether to request permission to download more than 200 MB or for all apps, tap the App downloads.

-Play videos automatically to view applications: Turn on automatic video playback

-Automatically remove unused applications: Turn off unused applications. You can reinstall the app at any time if it is still available in the App Store.

Set Content Limits and Avoid In-App Purchases

After turning on content and privacy restrictions, do the following.

1.Go to Settings> Screen Time> Content and Privacy Restrictions> Content Restrictions.

2.Set the following restrictions:

-iTunes and App Store Purchases: Check app installations, delete apps, and in-app purchases.

-Applications: Limit applications by age.

-Application clips: Prevents application clips from opening.

CHAPTER EIGHT

EVERYDAY APPS

Gather information about health and fitness in the Health app on iPhone

The Health app can track your daily steps and climbing steps.

You can manually add other information such as body weight and caffeine intake, and track additional data using other apps (such as nutrition and fitness apps)

and Health compatible devices such as Apple Watch, AirPods, scales, and blood pressure monitors.). , all sold separately).

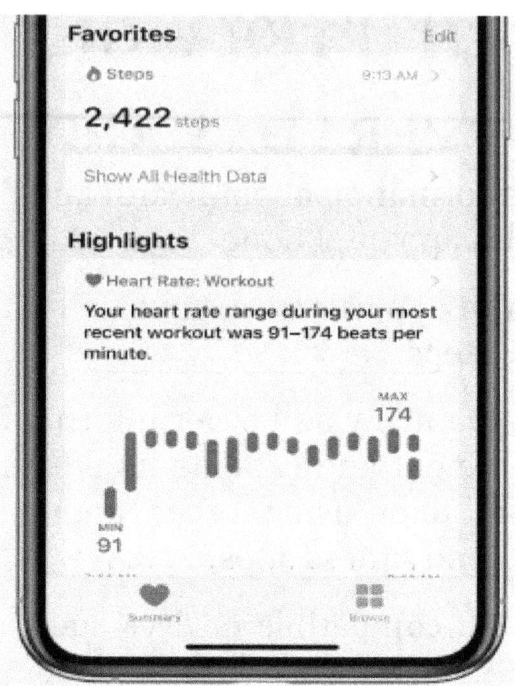

Manually add information to the health category

1.Tap Browse in the lower right corner to display the Health Category screen, and then do one of the following:

. Touch category. (To see all categories, scroll down.)

. Tap the search box, then enter a category name (such as body size) or a specific data type (such as weight).

If you do not see the Health Category screen, tap Review again in the lower right corner.

2.Touch the Details button for the data you want to update.

3.Tap Add data in the top right corner of the screen.

4.Add information, then tap Add or Done in the top right corner of the screen.

See Details In Health Categories

Tap Browse in the lower right corner to display the Health Category screen, and then do one of the following:

-Touch category.

-Tap the search box, then enter a category name (such as Body Measurement) or specific data types (such as temperature).

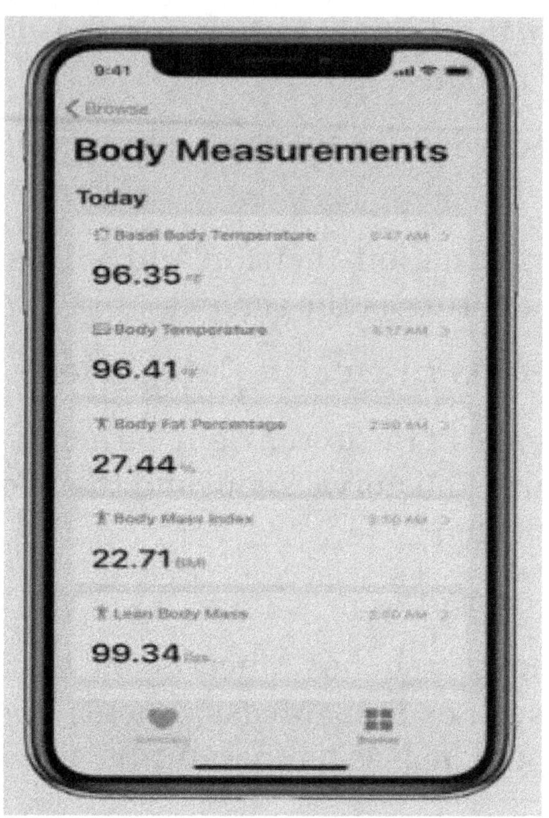

Detailed screen for Body Measurement category.

To view details of any data, click the Details button.

-View weekly, monthly, and annual data views: Tap the tabs at the top of the screen.

-Enter the data manually: Tap Add data in the upper right corner of the screen.

-Move the data type to Favourites on the screen Summary: Turn on Add to Favourites. (Scroll down if you don't see Add to Favourites.)

-See which apps and devices are allowed to share data: Touch Data Sources and Access under Options.

-To delete data: Tap Show all data below options, swipe left on the data entry, and then tap Delete To delete all data, tap Edit, then tap Delete all.

-Change the unit of measurement: Tap Unit under Options, then select another unit.

Menstrual Cycle iPhone

In the Health app, follow the menstrual cycle to get predictions for period and fertility.

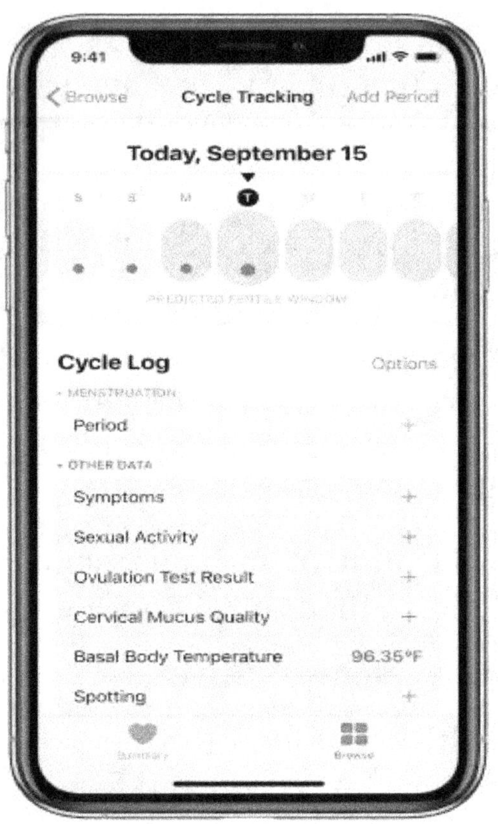

Start following the cycle

1.Tap Browses in the lower right corner, then tap Cycle Tracking.

2.Touch Start, then follow the on-screen instructions.

To help improve your forecast for the period and fertility period, enter the required information about the last period.

Make A Note of the Cycle Information

1.Tap Browses in the lower right corner, then tap Cycle Tracking.

2.Do one of the following:

-Note the day of the period: Tap the day in the calendar at the top of the screen. To record the flow level for that day, tap the Period under the Log Cycle, then select an option.

Or tap Add period in the top right corner, then select days from the monthly calendar.

Marked days are marked on the calendar with a solid red circle. To remove a recorded day, tap it.

-. Record Symptoms: Drag the calendar to the top of the screen to select a day, tap Symptoms, and then select everything that applies. When you're done, tap Done. Symptomatic days are represented by purple spots.

-Log detection: Drag the calendar to select a day, tap Spot, select Spot, and then tap Done.

3.To add extra categories, like ovulation test results and basic body temperature, click options, and then select categories.

Look at the fertility window period and forecasts

Tap Browses in the lower right corner, then tap Cycle Tracking.

The calendar shows the forecasts for your cycle along with the information you have previously recorded. The information shows in this format:

-Light red circles: predict your period.

To hide or show the days of the forecast period, tap Options, then turn the forecast period on or off.

-Clear blue days: Predict you're likely fertility window. Fertility predictions should not be used as a form of birth control.

To show or hide the Fertility window forecast, tap Options, then turn the Fertility forecast on or off.

-Solid red circles: Days on which you recorded a period.

-Purple spots: The days you registered for symptoms.

To select different days, drag the timeline. The data you recorded for the selected day is shown below in the cycle log.

Cycle Factor Management

1.Click Browses in the lower right corner and then click Cycle Tracking.

2.Scroll down, then tap Factors.

3.Do one of the following:

- Set a factor: Select any factor that currently applies to you, then tap Done.

-To add a factor: Click add factor, select a factor, click Start if you need to change the start date, and then click add.

-Change the end date to the current factor: Tap factor, tap Done, select date, then tap Done.

-To delete the current factor: Touch Factor, then tap Delete Factor.

-View records of previous features: Touch Show All.

Change period and fertility notifications and other cycle monitoring options

1.Tap Browses in the lower right corner, then tap Cycle Tracking.

2.Scroll down, then tap Options.

3.To switch an option on or off, click it.

See cycle history and statistics

1.Tap Browses in the lower right corner, then tap Cycle Tracking.

2.Scroll down to see the periods for your three most recent periods; scroll further to see related statistics.

3.To see more details and older information for Cycle History or Statistics, tap the Details button in that part of the screen.

To find just days that match a particular symptom or flow level in the Detailed Cycle History, tap Filters in the top right corner, select an option, and then tap Done.

Set Your First Sleep Schedule

You can set a schedule for waking up, wrapping, and going to bed for one or more days a week.

1.Tap Browses in the lower right corner, then tap Sleep.

2.Swipe up, then tap Start (under the Sleep settings).

3.Follow the on-screen instructions.

Replace The Next Alarm

You can temporarily change your sleep schedule.

1.Tap Browses in the lower right corner, then tap Sleep.

2.Scroll down to your Schedule, then tap Edit (under Next).

3.To adjust your sleep and wake schedule, drag the Sleep and Wake buttons.

4.Select alarm options:

. Turn on the alarm and turn it on or off.

. Choose sound or vibration.

5.Touch Done.

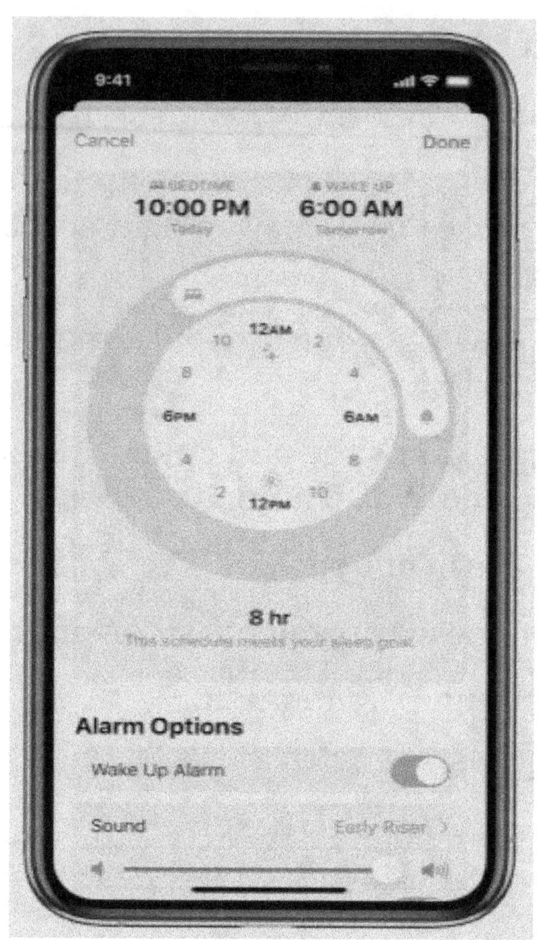

Note: You can also use the Clock application to change the next alarm.

After the next alarm goes off, your normal schedule resumes.

Change or add a sleep schedule

1.Tap Browses in the lower right corner, then tap Sleep.

2.Scroll down to your schedule, then tap Full Schedule and options.

3.Do one of the following:

-Change your sleep schedule: Tap Edit for the schedule you want to change.

-Add a sleep schedule: Tap Add a schedule for other days.

4.Do one of the following:

-Set days for your schedule: Tap the day at the top of the screen to add or remove it from your schedule. The schedule only applies to days shown in a solid circle.

-Adjust your sleep and wake-up schedule: Drag the Sleep button and the Wake button.

-Set alarm options: Turn the Alarm Alarm on or off.

When the wake-up alarm is turned on, you can select the sound, volume, and more.

-**Stop a sleep schedule**: Click remove list at the edge of the screen to erase an existing list or click cancel at the top of the screen to stop the new one.

5.When finished, tap Done or Add.

To turn off all sleep schedules, tap Browses in the lower right corner, tap Sleep, tap Full Schedule & Options, and then turn off Sleep Schedule (at the top of the screen).

Change the Wind Down schedule and activities

Tap Browses in the lower right corner, tap Sleep, tap Full Schedule & Options, and then do one of the following:

-Change when you turn on the sleep mode before the scheduled sleep time: Tap Wind Down, and then select a time.

-Add or remove winding activity: Tap Cut Shortcuts, and then tap Add another shortcut or the Delete button.

Pull switches for activities such as reading or listening to music appear on the lock screen when the iPhone is in sleep mode.

Change your sleep goal and other options

1.Tap Browses in the lower right corner, tap Sleep, and then tap Full Schedule & Options.

2.To change the sleep destination, tap the sleep destination, and then select a time.

3.To turn on or off other options, tap Options.

Do Not Disturb settings apply when the iPhone is in sleep mode. You can change these settings; for example, you can let calls go through selected contacts. See Do Not Disturb Setup on iPhone.

See the history of sleep

Healthy sleep data provides insight into your sleeping habits.

1.Tap Browses in the lower right corner, then tap Sleep.

2.Do one of the following:

-View sleep information by week or month: Tab at the top of the screen.

-Change the time range shown in the table: Drag the graph to the left or right.

-See the details of the day: Tap the column for the day.

-To add sleep information manually: Tap Add information in the upper right corner of the screen.

-Get summative sleep data: Click show more sleep data.

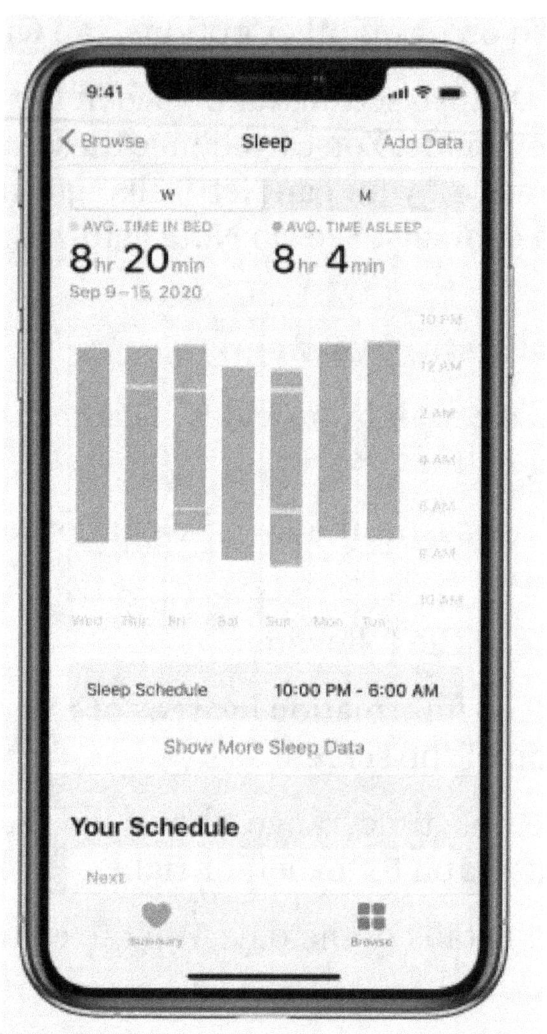

Time in bed reflects the period while lying in bed to sleep.

iPhone automatically tracks your time in bed by analyzing when you take and use an iPhone.

You can also click Options at the bottom of the screen, switch off Track Time in Bed and manually enter your estimated time in bed.

Or you can use a sleep tracking app or a connected sleep monitor to more easily determine how long you've been in bed.

Recording Voice Memo

A new option to improve recording is a one-touch feature that tries to improve the quality of your recording. It does this by using machine learning to remove potentially unwanted sounds such as background noises and echoes.

The result isn't always so dramatic and may not be particularly desirable for what you're recording, but it's worth a try and you can easily undo the improvements if you don't like it. Here you have to do both.

How to improve voice memo recordings?

1.Launch the Voice Memos app on your iOS device.

2.Record a new audio track or tap an existing track.

3.Touch the ellipse icon (three dots) that appears in the lower-left corner of the selected image.

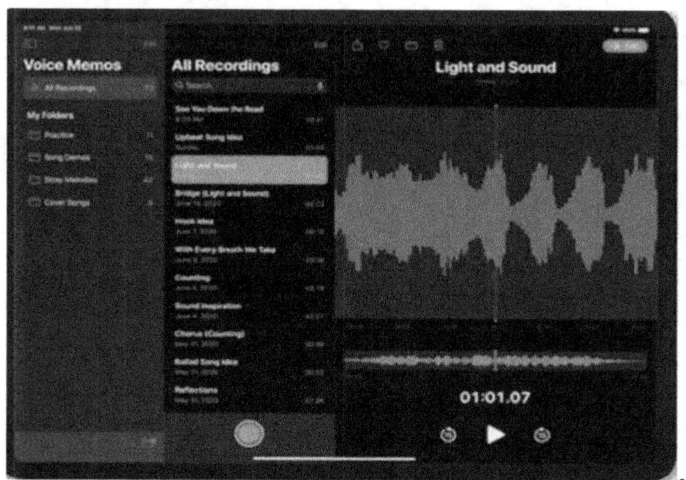

Select edit Recording on the voice menu.

5.Tap the magic wand icon in the top left corner of the screen.

6.Touch Done.

Now try touching the Play button on the selected sound - hopefully you hear a quality improvement. If not or it sounds worse to you, removes the extension by following the steps below.

How to Remove Voice Memo Enhancement?

1.Launch the Voice Memos app on your iOS device.

2.Select an existing recording.

3.Touch the ellipse icon (three dots) that appears in the lower-left corner of the selected image.

4.Select Edit Recording from the Actions menu.

5.Tap the magic wand icon in the upper left corner of the screen to remove it.

6.Touch Done.

Following the steps above, the sound sounds identical to the original recording.

Start with the news on an iPhone

-The News app collects all the stories you want to read from your favorite sources on the topics that interest you most.

To personalize News, you can select from a set of publications (called channels) and themes like Entertainment, Food, and Science, etc.

-The more you read, the better the news will understand your interests. Siri finds out what's important to you and suggests stories you might like. You can also receive notifications of important stories from the channels you follow.

-You can also subscribe to Apple News +, which includes hundreds of magazines, popular newspapers, and major digital publishers.

Note: To use News, you need Wi-Fi or a mobile connection. News and Apple News + are not available in all countries, regions, or languages.

Personalize Your News

When you follow a channel or topic, related stories appear more often in the Today feed, and the channel or topic appears in the Next tab.

1.Open News for the first time, click Follow, and then click button next to the channel and topic you want.

-If there are channels or topics you don't want to appear in your feed, tap the More button to block them or prevent News from suggesting them.

-When you block a channel or topic, its stories are filtered by the Today feed and the Today widget. However, you can view stories from channels you have blocked in Top Stories and other sites that contain stories selected by Apple News editors. Touch Tracking> Blocked Channels and Themes to view the channels and themes you have blocked.

2.Tap the Channel and find the theme at the bottom of the screen, then tap the Follow button for each channel and theme you want to follow.

-To stop tracking channels or topics, bring them to the left, then tap Cancel tracking.

-To easily track specific channels and topics, tap the search box at the top of the screen, enter a name for the channel or topic, and then tap the Follow button in the results below.

Get Notifications

Some channels you follow may send notifications of important stories.

1.Tap Tracking, switch to the bottom of the screen and then tap Notifications and email under Manage.

2.Turn on notifications for the desired channels.

If you subscribe to Apple News +, you can receive notifications when new issues become available. If you turn on Apple News Today, you get a link to the show notes related to the Apple News Today episode while listening to that episode.

Receive Apple Newsletters

You could select to get recent newsletters in your inbox on News editors.

1.Click Tracking, switch to the bottom of the screen, and then tap Notifications and email.

2.Slide to the bottom of the screen and then switch on Apple News.

To stop receiving newsletters, return to the Notifications and Email screen, and then turn off Apple News.

Note: Personalized newsletters are not available in all countries or regions.

Watch the stories only from the channels you follow

Go to Settings, tap News, turn Restrict Stories to Today, and then confirm your choice.

Note: The restriction of stories significantly limits the variety of stories that appear in Today's stuff and all other stuff. For instance, if you limit stories and take only one entertainment-related channel, your entertainment theme will contain stories from that channel only. When you limit stories, you don't see Top Stories and Trending Stories.

See selected news for you only on iPhone

Today's feed in the News application presents the main stories selected by the editors of Apple News, the best stories from the channels and topics it follows, as well as stories and editions from Apple News +. Depending on your location, today feed may also include audio news from Apple news and weather forecasts.

Note: Audio briefings for Apple News Today and local news and weather forecasts are not available in all countries or regions.

Access stories in the Today feed

1.Read more news in the group: Tap the arrow at the bottom of the group.

2.Video playback: Touch the Play button in the thumbnail.

-The linked article opens and the video plays.

3.Get the latest news: Flip down to refresh stuff Today with the latest stories.

Follow, revoke tracking, block and unblock channels and topics

You can control what is seen in today's feed by blocking channels and topics.

1.Do one of the following:

-Open channel feed: Tap and hold the story, then tap Go to channel. Or tap the story in the Today feed, then tap the channel name at the top of the story.

-Open topic feed: Tap a topic title - for example, movies or travel.

2.At the top of the feed, do one of the following:

-Follow: Tap the Follow button.

-Stop tracking: Tap the More button, and then tap Cancel channel tracking or Cancel subject tracking.

-Block: Tap the More button, then tap Channel block or Theme block.

-Unlock: Tap the More button, then tap Unlock Channel or Unlock Subject.

Tell News which stories you prefer

1.Touch Today.

2.Touch and hold the title, then tap Suggest more like this or Suggest less like this.

CHAPTER NINE

RELAXING WITH YOUR DEVICE

Around iTunes store

In the App Store, you can manage subscriptions and view and download purchases made by you or other family members.

You can also set limits and adjust your App Store settings in Setting.

Change The App Store Settings

Go to Settings> App Store, then do one of the following:

-Automatically download purchased applications on another Apple device: Under Applications automatically, turn on Applications below.

-Update applications automatically: Turn on app updates.

-Control the use of mobile data for application downloads: To allow downloads to use mobile data, turn on Automatic Download (under Mobile Data). To choose whether to request permission to download more than 200 MB or for all apps, tap the App downloads.

-Play videos automatically to view applications: Turn on automatic video playback.

-Automatically remove unused applications: Turn off unused applications on.

You can reinstall the app at any time if it is still available in the App Store.

Buying Items

Find music, movies, and TV shows

1.In the iTunes Store, click one of these:

- ✓ Music, or TV shows: Search by category. To change your browsing, click Genres at the up of the screen.
- ✓ Charts: See what's popular on iTunes.
- ✓ Search: Enter what you're looking for, then tap Search on your keyboard.
- ✓ More: Review the recommendations based on what you bought in iTunes.

2.Click an item to view more information about it. You can preview songs, watch movie and TV announcements, or Press the Share knob to do one of these below:

- Share a link to an article: Select a share option.
- Give an item as a gift: Tap the Gift.
- Add an item to your wish list: Touch Add to Wish List.

To view the wish list, tap the Item List button, then tap Wish List

Buy and Download Content

1.To buy an item, tap the price. If the item is free, tap Download.

If you see the Download button instead of the price, you have already purchased the item and can download it again free of charge.

2.If necessary, verify your Apple ID with a Face ID, Touch ID, or password to complete your purchase.

3.To see the download progress, click More and then click Downloads.

-Adjust the volume: Drag the volume slider.

Slide to an artist, album, or playlist: click the artist name under the song title, and then go to the artist, album, or playlist.

Drag to any point in the song: Drag the head of the game.

View timed texts

> ➤ Time-synchronized lyrics appear for many songs in Apple Music.
> ➤ Touch the player to open "Currently playing". The lyrics move in line with the music.
> ➤ To hide the text, press the Text button.

Tips & Warnings Tap certain lyrics - for example, the first line of a chorus - to skip to that part of the song.

To view all the lyrics, tap the More button, then tap View full song.

Note: You need an Apple Music subscription to view the lyrics.

Open the Control Centre, and then click the sound card.

Stream music to devices that support Bluetooth or AirPlay

1.Touch the player to open "Currently playing".

2.Touch the Play Destination button, then select the device.

Turn on Ask to Buy for kids on iPhone

When you set up Family Sharing, the family organizer can ask the children in the family group to ask permission to buy or download it for free. Purchases can be approved by the organizer or by a parent or guardian in the family group.

1.Launch Settings> your name> Family Sharing.

2.Click Ask to buy, and then do one of the these:

> If there are no children in your family group: Tap Add child or Open child account and then follow the on-screen instructions.
> If the child is in your family group: Tap the child's name, then turn on Ask to Buy.

READING

Read now: Touch to access the books and audiobooks you are currently reading. Slide down to see the books and audiobooks you Want to Read and the books you sampled. You can also set daily reading goals and keep track of the books you complete throughout the year.

Library: Touch to view all books, audiobooks, series, and PDFs you have received from the Book Store or manually added to the library. You can tap Collections to view your selected books in collections, such as I Want to Read, My Samples, Audio Books, and Done.

Read a book

Click the Read Now tab or the Library, and then click the cover to open the book. Use gestures to navigate these:

1.Rotate the page: Tap the right side of the page or flip right to the left.

2.Return to previous page: Tap the left side of the page or swipe from left to right.

3.Launch a specific page: click the page and move the slider at the bottom of the screen to the left or right. Or click the Search button and enter the page number, and then click the page number in the search results.

4.To close a book: Click the center of the page to display the controls, and then click the Back button.

Change the look of the text and display

Tap the page, tap the Appearance button, and then do one of the following:

1.Adjust the brightness of the screen: Drag the slider to the left or right.

2.Change font size: Touch major A to increase the font size or touch lowercase A to decrease it.

3.Change the font: Touch Fonts to select another font.

4.To change the background color of a page: Tap a colored circle.

5.Turn the screen on when dark: Turn on the automatic night theme to automatically change the color and brightness of the page when using Books in low light conditions.

6.Turn off pagination: Turn on the vertical scroll to scroll continuously from a book or PDF.

Bookmark The Page

When you close a book, your post is automatically saved - you don't have to add a bookmark. Highlight the pages you want to return to.

-Click the bookmark ribbon to add a bookmark; tap again to remove the bookmark.

-To view all bookmarks, tap the Contents button, and then tap Bookmarks.

Highlight or underline the text

1.Touch and hold a word, then move the capture points to adjust the selection.

2.Touch Highlight and then touch the Highlight Color Chooser button to select the color to highlight or underline.

To remove an emphasis or emphasis, tap the text, and then tap the Trash button.

To view all your highlighted items, tap the Content button, and then tap Notes.

Add a note

1.Touch and hold a word, then move the capture points to adjust the selection.

2.Click Note, use the keyboard to enter text, and then click Done.

To view all notes, tap the Contents button, then tap Notes. Slide left on the note to erase it.

Share The Choice

You can send text selections using AirDrop, Mail, or Messages, or you can add selections to Notes. If the book is from a Book Store, a link to the book is included with the selection. (This provision may not be available in all countries or regions).

1.Touch and hold a word, then move the capture points to adjust the selection.

2.Touch Share, then select a method.

You can also send a link to view the book at the bookstore. Tap any page, tap the Content button, and then tap the Share button.

Access Your Books On All Devices

To update your book information on iPhone, iPad, and iPod touch, sign in with the same Apple ID on each device, and then do the following:

- o Sync your reading position, bookmarks, notes, and highlights: Go to Settings> [your name]> iCloud, then turn on iCloud Drive and Books.
- o Sync read now, library and collections: Go to Settings> [your name]> iCloud and turn on iCloud Drive and Books. Then go to Settings> Books and turn on Reading Nov.

CHAPTER TEN

ON THE GO

Set the location sharing

1.Touch me, then turn on Share My Location.

The device that crosses your location is shown under My Location.

2.If your iPhone does not currently share your location, scroll to the bottom, then tap Use this iPhone as my location

Set A Label for Your Location

You can set a label for your current location to make it more meaningful (such as home or work). When you touch me, you see a sticker near the place.

1.Tap Me, then tap Edit location name.

2.Choose a label.

To add a new bookmark, tap 'Add a custom bookmark, enter a name, then tap Done.

Share your location with a friend

1.Touch People.

2.Scroll to the bottom of the People list, then tap Share my location.

3.In the to field, enter the name of the friend you want to share your location with (or tap the Add Contact button and select a contact).

4.Tap Submit and select how long it takes to cross your location.

When location changes notify your family member or a friend.

If you are a member of a family-sharing group, see Share your location with family members.

Stop sharing your location

You can stop sharing the place with a certain friend or hide from everyone.

- Stop sharing with a friend: Tap People, then tap the name of the person you don't want to share with your location. Tap Stop Sharing My Location and then tap Stop Sharing Location.
- Hide your area from everyone: Click me, and then switch off Share my location.

Respond to the request to share the place

1.Touch People.

2.Tap Share under the name of the friend who sent the request and selects how long to share your location.

If you do not want to share your location, tap Cancel.

Don't stop receiving new requests for location sharing

Touch me, then turn off Leave friends requests.

See a friend's place

Tap People, then tap the name of the person you want to find.

1.If your friend can be found: Appear on the map so you can see where they are.

2.If your friend can't be found: Under his name, you see "No place found."

3.If you don't follow your friend: Under their name, you see "He can see your location". You can ask to see a friend's place.

You can also ask Siri to find a friend who shares their location with you.

Ask Siri. Say something like, "Where's Sarah?" Learn how to ask Siri.

Contact A Friend

1.Tap People, then tap the name of the person you want to contact.

2.Tap Contact and select how you want to contact your friend.

Find directions to a friend

You can get directions to your friends' current location in the Maps app.

1.Tap People, then tap the name of the person you want to get directions to.

2.Touch Instructions to open Maps.

3.Click the route to get directions from your recent location to your friend's location.

Set a friend's place tag

You can tag a friend's current location to make it more meaningful (like home or work). The label appears under your friend's name when they are at that location.

1.Click People and then click the name of the person you want to placemark on.

2.Touch Edit the place name, then select a tag.

3.To add a new bookmark, tap Add a custom bookmark, enter a name, then tap Done.

Mark favorite friends

Favorite friends appear at the top of the People list and are marked with an asterisk.

1.Tap People, then find the person you want to mark as a favorite.

2.Do one of the following:

-Touch the person's name, then tap Add [name] to Favorites.

-Swipe left on the person's name, then tap an asterisk.

-To remove a friend from favorites, swipe left and tap asterisk or tap friend, then tap Remove [name] from favorites.

WALLET

Wallet app could use to keep prizes, passes, event tickets all together in one place, and more for easy access.

Steps can contain useful information, such as coffee card status, coupon expiration date, or boarding information.

Add A Pass

You may be asked to add a step to the app after acting such as purchasing a ticket. Or you can press add to Apple Wallet when you see the following:

1.Wallet-enabled applications

2.Mail or Messages

3.Web browser like Safari

4.AirDrop sharing

5.Wallet notification after using Apple Pay with a supported retailer

6.QR or bar code

To scan the code, open the Camera app, then set the iPhone so that the code appears on the screen.

Rearrange The Passages

1.In the Wallet row, tap and hold the pace you want to move.

2.Drag the path to a new location in the row.

The step order is updated on the iPhone, iPod touch, and Apple Watch where you are logged in with your Apple ID.

Review the step information and change its settings

1.Tap the step and then tap the More button.

2.Select any of the following (not all options are available on all passes):

-Automatic update: Allow passes to receive updates from the publisher.

-Suggest on the lock screen: Show the passage based on time or place.

To allow access to a location, go to Settings> Privacy> Location Services> Wallet, then tap While using the app.

-Automatic selection: Select the passage where necessary.

-Share Step: Send a step to a friend using Mail or Messages.

-Remove step: Remove the step from all devices where you signed in with your Apple ID.

3.Scroll down to see other information, such as the associated application, usage details, and terms and conditions.

Change The Settings For All Passes

1.Update through another device regularly: Sign in with your Apple ID on iPhone, iPod touch, and Apple Watch.

Note: This setting only applies to wallet passes, not to cards you use with Apple Pay.

2.Set notification options: Go to Settings> Notifications> Wallet.

3.Prevent the passwords from appearing on the lock screen:

Go to Settings> Wallet and Apple Pai, then turn off the Double-Click side button (on iPhone with Face ID) or Double-Click Home (on models other than iPhone)

SPEAKING THEIR LANGUAGE

Translate text or your voice

1.Turn the iPhone to a photo orientation, then tap the Translate tab.

2.Select the languages you want to translate from at the top of the screen.

3.Tap Enter text, type a phrase, and then tap Go. Or tap the Listen button and say the phrase.

4.When the translation is displayed, do one of the following:

-. Play the sound of the translation again: Touch the Play button.

-Save the translation in the Favorites tab: Tap the Star button.

-Lookup a word in the dictionary: Tap the Dictionary button, then tap a word to see its definition.

You can also view recent history and save newly translated phrases in the Favorites tab.

Translate the conversation

Here, the screen of your phone will split to show both transcribed and translated text on two sides of the dialogue, with a translated tone. Talk mode works for downloaded languages even when you do not connect to the internet.

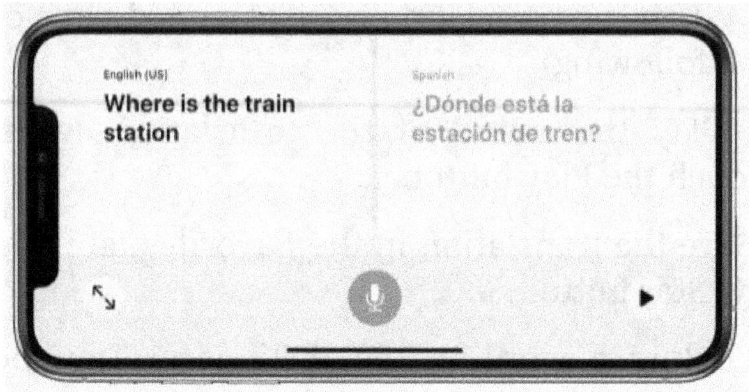

1.On the Translation tab, rotate the iPhone horizontally.

2.Touch the Listen button and then speak one of the two languages.

Download languages on iPhone for offline translation

1.Tap the Translator tab, then tap the language at the top of the screen.

2.Scroll down to Available Offline Languages, tap the languages you want to download, then tap Done.

CHAPTER ELEVEN

CAMERAS AND PHOTOS

Record a QuickTake video

QuickTake video is a video recorder in photo mode. While recording a QuickTake video, you can move the Record button to the locked position and continue recording photos.

1.In photo mode, touch and hold the shutter button to start recording QuickTake videos.

2.Move the shutter button to the right and slide the hands-free lock.

Both the Capture button and the Shutter button appear below the frame - tap the Shutter button to take a photo while shooting.

3.Touch the Record button to stop recording.

Tips & Warnings Press and hold the volume up or down button to start recording QuickTake videos in photo mode.

4.Tap the thumbnail to watch the QuickTake video in the Photos app.

Record Video Slowly

You can record a video in Slo-mo mode, and also edit your video so that the slow-motion starts and stops at a specified time.

1.Select Slo-mo mode.

On the iPhone 11 and iPhone 12, you can touch the Camera Chooser Back-Facing button to shoot in Slo-mo mode with the front camera.

2.Touch the Record button or press any volume button to start recording.

You can touch the shutter button to take a photo while shooting.

3.Touch the Record button or press any volume button to stop recording.

To play the part of the video slowly and the rest to play at a regular speed, click the video thumbnail, and then click Edit. Move the vertical bars under the frame viewer to define the section you want to play slowly.

Turn The Scene Detection On And Off

1.On iPhone 12 models, the scene detection setting can identify objects in different scenes and enhance them automatically.

2.Scene recognition is activated automatically. To switch off Scene Detection, launch Settings> Camera, and then switch off Scene Detection.

Take A Look at Your Photos

1.In the camera, tap the thumbnail in the lower-left corner.

2.Swipe left or right to view recently taken photos.

3.Tap the screen to show or hide the controls.

4.Touch All Photos to view all your photos and videos saved in Photos.

Share And Print Photos

1.While viewing a photo, tap the Share button.

2.Choose an option such as AirDrop, Mail, or Messages to share your photo.

3.Swipe up to select Print from the list of actions.

The camera can Scan QR code

With a Camera or Code Scanner, you can scan QR codes for links to websites, apps, coupons, maps, and more. The camera automatically detects and highlights the QR code.

1.Open the Camera, and then set the phone so that the code shows on the screen.

2.Click the notification that shows on the screen to go to the appropriate website or app.

Open the Code Scanner from the Control Center

1.Go to Settings> Control Center, then tap the Insert button next to the Scanner code.

2.Open the Control Center, tap Code Scanner, and then set the iPhone so that the code appears on the screen.

3.To add more lights, tap the flashlight to turn it on.

Live Photo Playback

The Live Photo Button Live Photo is a moving image that takes moments immediately before and after shooting.

1.Open the live photo.

2.Touch and hold a photo to play it back.

See Capture a live photo.

Take a look at the photos in the burst shot

Quick shooting mode The camera takes many high-speed photos so you can select a full range of photos. In Photos, the Burst Burst is stored together in a single photo frame. You can preview each photo one after the other, then select your favorites to save them separately.

1.Open the Burst photo.

2.Touch Select, then flip the photo collection.

3.To save specific photos, click each photo to select it, and then click Done.

4.Touch Hold All to keep the bursts and photos you have selected, or touch Hold only [Number] of Favorites to keep only the ones you have selected.

Playing The Video

As you browse the photo library on the Library tab, videos play automatically as you move. Touch a video to start playing a full screen without sound, and then do one of the following:

1.Click the player controls below the video to stop, play, turn on and turn off the sound; tap the screen to hide the player controls.

2.Double-tap the screen to switch between full screen and custom screen.

Play and customize the presentation

The slide show is a collection of your photos, formatted and set to music.

1.Click the Library tab.

2.Browse photos from All Photos or Daisy, then tap Select.

3.Touch each photo you want to include in the slideshow and then touch the Share button.

4.In the list of options, click Slideshow.

5.Tap the screen, then tap Options in the lower right corner to change the presentation theme, music, and more.

Adjust light and color

In the Photos app, tap a photo or video thumbnail to view it in full screen.

1.Touch Edit, then swipe left under the photo to see buttons for editing each effect, such as Exposure, Brilliance, and Highlights.

2.Touch the button, then drag the slider to adjust the effect.

3.The adjustment level for each effect is shown by the outlines around the button, so you can see at a glance which effects are increasing or decreasing.

4.To predict an effect, press the effect button to see the shot before and after applying the effect (or tap a photo to switch between the edited and original version).

5.Tap Done to save the changes, or if you don't like the changes, tap Cancel, then tap Reject changes.

Tips & Warnings Touch the Enhance button to automatically edit photos or videos with effects.

Crop, flip rotate a photo and video

1.In the Photos app, tap a photo or video thumbnail to view it in full screen.

2.Click Edit, click, and then do one of the following:

-Crop manually: Push the edge of the rectangle to close the area you want to hold in the photo, or you can pinch open or closed.

-Cut to the preset ratio: Touch the Standard Crop button, then select a ratio such as square, 2: 3, 8:10, and more.

-Rotate: Touch the Rotate button to rotate the photo 90 degrees.

-Flip: Touch the Flip button to flip the image horizontally.

3.Click Done to save the changes, or if you don't like the changes, tap Cancel, then tap Reject changes.

Correct and adjust perspective

1.In the Photos app, tap a photo or video thumbnail to view it in full screen.

2.Click Edit and then click.

3.Select the effect button to align, adjust the vertical perspective, or adjust the horizontal perspective.

4.Drag the slider to adjust the effect.

-The adjustment level for each effect is shown in yellow outlines around the button, so you can see at a glance which effects are added or subtracted. Touch the button to switch between the edited and original effect.

5.Touch Done to save your changes.

Apply filter effects

1.In the Photos app, tap a photo or video thumbnail to view it in full screen.

2.Tap Edit and then tap the Filters button to apply filter effects such as Vivid, Dramatic, or Silverstone.

3.Touch the filter, then drag the slider to adjust the effect.

4.To compare the edited photo with the original, tap.

5.Tap Done to save the changes, or if you don't like the changes, tap Cancel, then tap Reject changes.

Restore the edited photo

After editing the photo and saving the changes, you can return to the original image.

1.Open the edited image, tap Edit, then tap Restore.

2.Touch Restore to the original.

Highlight a photo

1.Touch a photo to view it on full screen.

2.Touch Edit and then tap the Extras button.

3.Tap Mark-up.

4.Add a photo with a variety of drawing and coloring tools. Tap the Add Notes button to add forms, text, or even your signature.

Cut the video

1.In the Photos app, open the video, then tap Edit.

2.Drag each end of the browser box, then tap Done.

3.Touch Save Video to save only the cut video or Save Video as New Clip to save both versions of the video.

To cancel trimming after saving, open the video, tap Edit, and then tap Restore.

Note: Video saved as a new recording cannot be returned to the original.

Adjust the slow-motion portion of the video recorded in Slo-mo

1.Open the video in Slo-mo, then tap Edit.

2.Drag the white vertical bars under the frame viewer to set where the video plays slowly.

Add effects to Live Photo

You can make changes to Live Photos to turn them into funny videos.

1.Open Live Photo.

2.Swipe up to see the effects, then select one of the following:

-Loop: Repeat the action in a continuous video.

-Bounce: rejects the action back and forth.

-Long exposure: Simulates a long exposure effect similar to DSLR through motion blur.

CHAPTER TWELVE

PRACTICAL MATTERS

Charging cable for iPhone

Your iPhone is part of these charging cables:

USB-C lightning cable

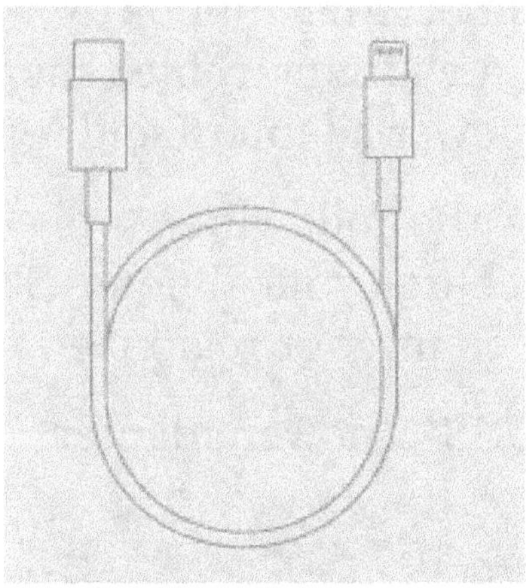

Lightning for the USB cable

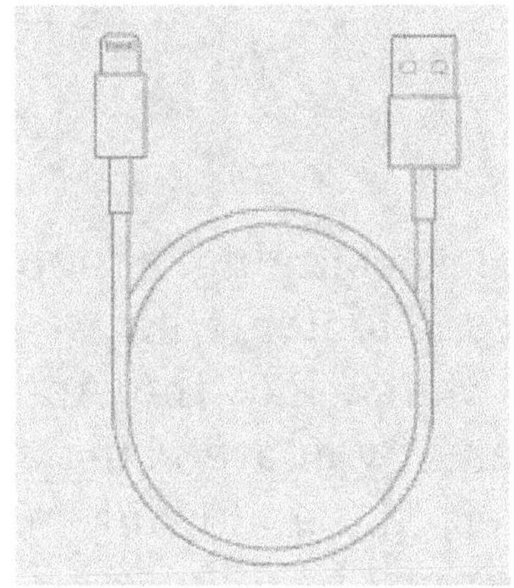

You can connect the iPhone to an electrical plug using a compatible power adapter (sold separately) and the included cable.

You can also connect this cable to a computer's USB port for charging and syncing.

Rectifiers for iPhone

You can connect the iPhone to an electrical outlet using a charging cable (supplied) and a compatible power adapter (sold separately).

You can use the following Apple USB power adapters to charge your iPhone. Size and style may vary by country or region.

Apple 20V USB-C power adapter

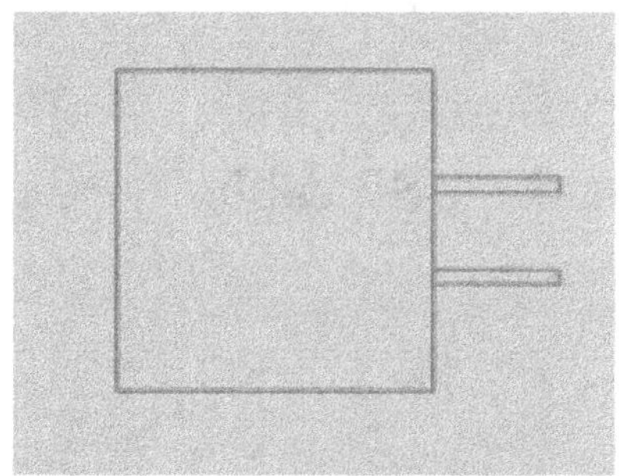

Note: For quick charging, iPhone 12 models need a power adapter with at least output power of 20 watts, like the Apple 20V USB power adapter. If you are using a stand-alone power adapter, the following recommended specifications must be followed:

1.Frequency: 50 to 60 Hz, single phase

2.Mains voltage: 100 to 240 VAC

3.Output voltage / current: 9 VDC / 2.2 A.

4.Minimum output power: 20 V

5.Output port: USB-C

Apple 18V USB-C power adapter

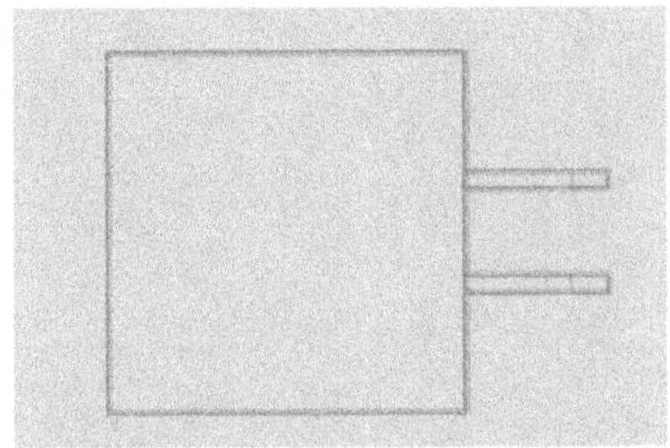

Apple 5V USB power adapter

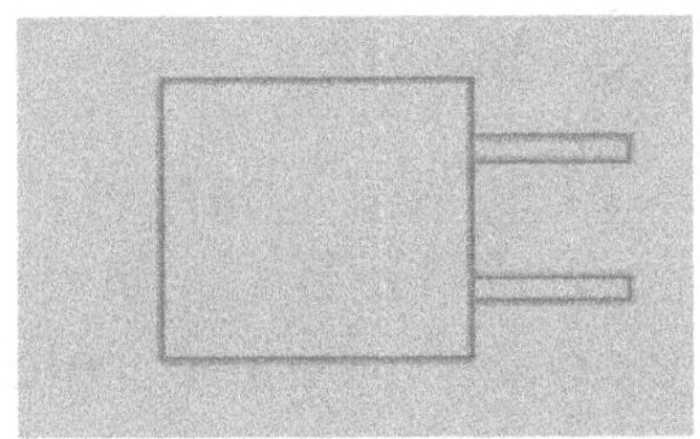

Apple USB power adapters can be used for iPad and Mac notebooks and you can also use standalone power adapters that comply with applicable state regulations and international and regional safety standards.

Mag-safe Chargers for iPhone

Charge iPhone with MagSafe charger

On iPhone 12 models, the MagSafe charger (sold separately) is placed magnetically on the back of the iPhone or the MagSafe box or case (sold separately) and properly aligns the iPhone, allowing you to hold and use the iPhone while charging.

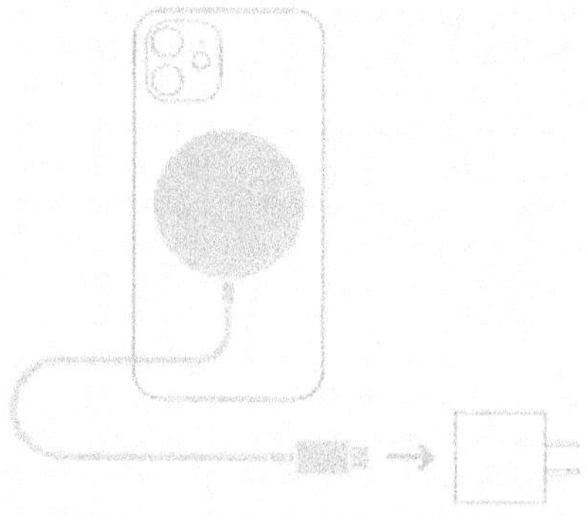

MagSafe charger with other models that support wireless charging.

1.Connect the MagSafe charger to the power with the Apple 20V USB-C power adapter. or another fitting power adapter (sold separately).

2.Do one of the following:

-iPhone 12 Models: Place the MagSafe charger on the back of the iPhone or its MagSafe case or sleeve. When the iPhone starts charging, a green charging symbol appears.

Note: If the iPhone's leather wallet is stuck, remove it before placing the MagSafe charger on the back of the box

CHAPTER THIRTEEN

HOW TO PROTECT YOUR PHONE FROM VIRUSES?

How to Remove Virus from iPhone

Some people think that iPhones never get viruses. They do, but very rarely.

If you think there's a virus on your iPhone, you may be right, but you're more likely to see an app that's behaving badly - which may be trying to convince you that iOS is infected.

If you're convinced that your iPhone or iPad has a virus or other form of malware, read on to find out if it's true, and if so, find how to remove it.

Ascertain If Your iPhone Has a Virus

Technically, a virus is a piece of code that enters into another program, while a worm is a stand apart program; two of them seek to share themselves by seizing or interrupting messaging applications or through social engineering.

The iOS platform has seen several attacks that fit the first definition when attackers entered malicious code into reputable applications or seized the development tool used to create them. Although compromised applications must be caught in the App Store approval phase, those who have corrupted their devices can download the applications from unofficial sources, which could mean they have inadvertently installed something dangerous.

However, the iOS sandbox structure can prevent a malware attack from affecting other applications

What causes the problem?

The main questions when trying to determine what happened to your iPhone or iPad that are not working properly are the following:

Did you take the device out of jail? And if so, did you install the application from an unofficial source whose authenticity is questionable? If the answer is both, you may have malware on your device and you should try to isolate and uninstall the culprit.

Does unexpected behavior appear when you only use certain applications? If that's the case - and especially if it's just one application - then you're probably looking for a problem related to a particular application and fixing it in a moment.

There are, however, alternative options.

For example, Intel's Mac Internet Security can scan viruses on an iOS device. Bitdefender Total Security is also an option for Mac and PC users to add protection for iOS devices, and throw a VPN into the combination.

If the problem persists no matter what apps are open, there's a good chance your device will behave badly because of a hardware problem or an iOS change you're not yet accustomed to, or because you or another user changed the device maybe unintentionally.

It is extremely unlikely that the malware penetrated the core of the operating system and caused system-wide problems; this would be essentially unprecedented. In each of these cases, we take the device to the Apple Genius Bar.

This does not necessarily mean that the application is wrong or that the developers are to blame; conversely, the fact that an application is made by a renowned company does not prevent it from being by hackers or malware.

Since hackers can't get into iOS itself, one of their most common strategies is to hack developers, who in turn can be used by unconscious app developers. The scammers are thus allowed to redirect you to a fictitious website when using an application created using a compromised tool.

It is usually obvious when the culprit is one particular application because you only have problems when using it. A common sign of donation is that when you open the app, you are sometimes redirected to a website or App Store without your permission.

If you think the problem is in one application, first see if an updated version of the application is available, because the problem may have been noticed and resolved. Also, check the application's website (if any) and/or Twitter feed developer (if any) to see if the problem has been reported or discussed in those posts.

If the developers are available to contact, you should report the problem to them. They may be able to offer a solution right away, but even if they can't, they are more likely to find a solution if they know about it.

Assuming that updating the application does not solve the problem, uninstall it and try to handle it without it for a while. If the problem ends, I've found the culprit and it's time to decide if you can do it in the long run without the app. Even if you decide to delete the application permanently, keep in mind that from time to time you can contact the developers and see if a satisfactory update has taken place.

Clear the history and data of the website

Here is a short tip that can solve problems with redirecting web pages. Go to Settings> Safari> Clear History and Website Information, then tap Clear History & Data to confirm.

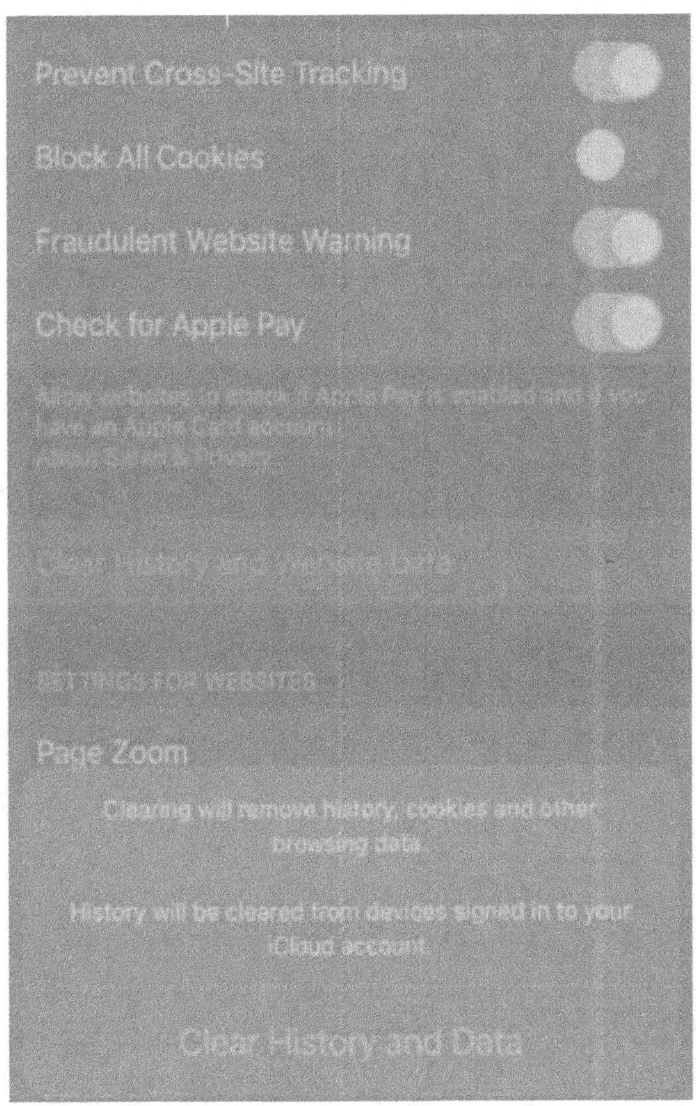

Shut down and restart

   ✓ -Hold down the power button until the screen changes and the shutdown slider appears. (This should take about four to five seconds.) Then move the slider to turn off the phone. The screen turns black.

- ✓ -On an iPhone without a Home button, like the iPhone 12 Pro, you need to hold the power button and the mute button at the same time.
- ✓ -To restart the phone, press and hold the power button again. This time it took about 10 seconds. The Apple logo appears; at this point, you can release the power button. Wait until the password entry screen appears (you must enter the password instead of using the Touch ID / Face ID the first time you open the phone after turning it on), and then open the device.
- ✓ Does this solve the problem? If no, do this.

Restore IPhone from Backup

We believe that you back up your iPhone regularly. If so, it will be easy to restore your iPhone from the last backup and see if the solution has been removed.

If this fails, you may have backed up the contents of your iPhone, including other problem malware, then restored it from the second most recent backup, then from the previous one, and so on. We hope to find a backup that dates the problem in advance and that you can continue from there.

Restore Your iPhone As A New Device

If no backup contains malware or only non-malware backups cannot be used for some other reason, it may be best to start from scratch.

Delete the iPhone by going to Settings> General> Reset> Delete All Content and Settings, then enter the password and confirm. Wait for the deletion to complete, then set up the iPhone as the new device.

We describe this process in more detail in separate articles: How to reset iPhone and How to set up a new iPhone.

When you're done setting up, you'll need to reinstall the apps you want to use (though keep in mind that if an app causes a problem, try living without it for a while and see if things get better), reload the songs, photos, and videos and restore the settings as you wish. It's painful, but I hope you only do it once.

How To Protect iPhone From Malware

Update iOS or iPadOS regularly. We recommend that you do not jailbreak, and if you do, you must be very careful about the software you install and the sources from which you download it. And watch out for "social engineering" attacks - don't open links if you're not sure where they're coming from.

You may also want to invest in antivirus for your iPhone. If you already have an antivirus for Mac, there's a good chance you have an iPhone app included in your subscription. Our recommendation for the iPhone would be Bitdefender

INDEX